**NEW DIRECTIONS
FOR CONTINUING
EDUCATION**

Number 9 • 1981

NEW DIRECTIONS FOR CONTINUING EDUCATION

A Quarterly Sourcebook
Alan B. Knox, Editor-in-Chief

Number 9, 1981

Strengthening Internal Support for Continuing Education

James C. Votruba
Guest Editor

Jossey-Bass Inc., Publishers
San Francisco • Washington • London

LC
5219
.S88

STRENGTHENING INTERNAL SUPPORT
FOR CONTINUING EDUCATION
New Directions for Continuing Education
Number 9, 1981
    James C. Votruba, Guest Editor

Copyright © 1981 by Jossey-Bass Inc., Publishers
               and
            Jossey-Bass Limited

Copyright under International, Pan American, and Universal
Copyright Conventions. All rights reserved. No part of
this issue may be reproduced in any form—except for brief
quotation (not to exceed 500 words) in a review or professional
work—without permission in writing from the publishers.

New Directions for Continuing Education (publication number
USPS 493-930) quarterly by Jossey-Bass Inc., Publishers.
Subscriptions are available at the regular rate for institutions,
libraries, and agencies of $30 for one year. Individuals may
subscribe at the special professional rate of $18 for one year.

Correspondence:
Subscriptions, single-issue orders, change of address notices,
undelivered copies, and other correspondence should be sent to
New Directions Subscriptions, Jossey-Bass Inc., Publishers,
433 California Street, San Francisco, California 94104.

Editorial correspondence should be sent to the Editor-in-Chief,
Alan B. Knox, Office for the Study of Continuing Professional
Education, University of Illinois at Urbana-Champaign,
Urbana, Illinois 61801.

Library of Congress Catalogue Card Number LC 80-84267
International Standard Serial Number ISSN 0195-2242
International Standard Book Number ISBN 87589-816-5

Cover design by Willi Baum
Manufactured in the United States of America

Contents

Editor's Notes   James C. Votruba   vii

The Continuing Education Agency and Its Parent Organization   Alan B. Knox   1

     A social system perspective is used to examine the interplay between the continuing education agency and its parent organization.

Strategies for Organizational Change   James C. Votruba   13

     Strengthening organizational support for continuing education is analyzed from the perspective of planned organizational change.

Strengthening the University Continuing Education Mission   Paul A. Miller   29

     The author draws upon his extensive experience to suggest steps to more fully develop continuing education as a primary university mission.

Strengthening Collegiate Financial Support for Continuing Education   Dennis A. Dahl   37
                                                                                              Robert G. Simerly

     The social system approach to planned change described in Chapter Two is used to develop a strategy for strengthening collegiate financial support.

Strengthening Collegiate Faculty Rewards for Continuing Education   Donald E. Hanna   43

     The author describes an attempt to integrate continuing education into the primary faculty reward system of a Midwestern land grant university.

Strengthening Collegiate Adult Student Services   Judith A. Riggs   51

     A strategy is suggested for increasing collegiate support for adult student support services.

Strengthening Continuing Education in Community Colleges   James F. Gollattscheck   57

     Community colleges can more fully develop their continuing education mission by adopting a more unified approach to meeting all the educational needs of the community.

Strengthening Public School Support   Hal Beder   **65**
for Continuing Education
>A practical strategy for increasing public school support for continuing education should emphasize the benefits to the school system from such programs.

Establishing Public School Programs for   Marion G. Marshall   **73**
Older Adults
>A process is described for establishing public school programs for older adults with special emphasis upon strengthening support for such programs.

Continuing Education in Libraries: Barbara Conroy   **81**
A Challenge to Change Agents
>The author suggests that public libraries must expand their continuing education involvement or risk loss of public support.

Strengthening Corporate Continuing   Martin E. Smith   **89**
Education: A Case History
>A strategy of centralization is described as a way to strengthen corporate training programs.

Regionalized Continuing Medical Education: Joseph S. Green   **97**
Building Multi-Institutional Support
>If Veterans Administration Regional Medical Education Centers are to be effective providers of continuing medical education, they need the support of VA hospitals and health care centers throughout the region.

A Final Note to Continuing Educators   James C. Votruba   **105**
Working as Change Agents
>The sourcebook editor summarizes the continuing educator's change agent role and offers some very practical advice.

Index   **109**

Editor's Notes

Continuing education agencies typically are part of larger parent organizations tht do not view education of adults as their primary mission. This often results in a peripheral status for continuing education, which in turn forces cntinuing educators to constantly struggle to sustain and expand their continuing education activities. To the extent that the continuing education agency is dependent upon the parent organization for budget, staffing, program approval, and other resource allocations, this struggle becomes both difficult and unavoidable, and continuing educators often find themselves ill prepared.

Strengthening organizational support for continuing education can take many forms. Often it involves trying to develop more informed and supportive attitudes on the part of key organizational administrators and policy makers concerning the importance of the continuing education mission. It also involves the need to challenge time-honored organizational traditions concerning who can teach, who can learn, and where, when, and how teaching and learning can take place. Inevitably, it also involves modifying organizational policies and procedures in order to better serve the educational needs of adults.

The purpose of this sourcebook is to examine the *process* through which continuing educators can stimulate support for continuing education within their parent organization. In this regard, the sourcebook perspective is to view the continuing educator as an organizational change agent whose task is not only to identify those organizational changes that need to occur but also to develop a well-designed and well-managed strategy for bringing them about. In short, the sourcebook objective is to assist continuing educators in becoming more effective leaders of organizational adaptation and change.

The first two chapters set the conceptual stage for examining the process of securing organizational support for continuing education. Chapter One uses an open systems perspective to describe the nature of the continuing education agency and its relationship with its parent organization. Chapter Two then discusses the organizational change process with special emphasis on the role of the continuing educator in the design and management of successful planned change strategies.

Chapters Three through Twelve examine specific approaches to strengthening continuing education support in a variety of organizational settings including universities, community colleges, public schools, libraries, large corporations, and complex multi-institutional systems. In these chapters, the authors describe efforts in which they have played a central change agent role.

Finally, Chapter Thirteen offers suggestions to continuing educators who intend to function as change agents within their parent organization.

In recent years, an abundance of prescriptive literature has been generated concerning the changes that need to occur in various types of organizations to make them more responsive to the lifelong education needs of adults. Unfortunately, an equally rich body of literature has not emerged concerning the process for bringing these changes about. This sourcebook helps correct this imbalance by relating some of the most recent and most exciting developments in planned change theory and practice to the organizational world in which continuing educators must function.

James C. Votruba
Editor

James C. Votruba is associate director of the Office of Continuing Education and Public Service and assistant professor of both continuing education and higher education, University of Illinois at Urbana-Champaign. He has written and consulted extensively in the area of strengthening support for continuing education within collegiate institutions.

*An understanding of relationships between a
continuing education agency and its parent
organization can help an administrator develop
effective strategies to increase organizational support.*

The Continuing Education Agency and Its Parent Organization

Alan B. Knox

Most continuing education administrators want to strengthen the relationship between their agency and its parent organization. In addition to effective personal interactions, an administrator's ability to strengthen this relationship can be enhanced by an understanding of the organizational dynamics of the parent organization as a social system and of the continuing education agency as a subsystem.

    Practitioners are typically aware of the unique features of their own agencies: distinctive histories, specific locations and staff members, and interrelationships with a parent organization and a service area. Each agency also shares characteristics with other agencies with the same type of parent organization and has organizational dynamics common to continuing education agencies in all settings. The purpose of this chapter is to highlight features of relationships with the parent organization that are common to most continuing education agencies and to note illustrative relationships that are important in various types of agencies.

    Effective administrators of continuing education agencies demonstrate the importance of constructive relationships with their parent organizations. Such relationships reflect an ability to obtain resources, use procedures, and produce results in ways that take the parent organization into account.

Continuing education agencies may be large (Cooperative Extension Service of a land-grant university or the education and training division of a large corporation), or they may be small (adult services office of a public library or the adult religious education office of a religious institution). Large or small, the subsystem is largely defined by the interdependent roles that are performed by administrators who coordinate the total effort, by resource persons who conduct the educational activities, by participants who engage in the learning activities, by support staff members who assist with secretarial and maintenance tasks, and by policy makers who influence the agency's priorities. Administrative leadership includes helping to achieve consensus on goals, encouraging contributions to the achievement of goals, and reducing undesirable role conflicts.

Many continuing education agencies are subsystems of such organizations as schools, community colleges, and universities. Educational organizations possess resources for learning, and the main purpose of the continuing education agency is to extend the availability of learning resources to adults. However, more than half of the continuing education in North America is provided by agencies that are not part of educational institutions, for examples, employers (business, industry, government, military), labor unions, religious institutions, libraries, museums, professional associations, hospitals, community organizations, and a variety of voluntary associations. The main purposes of noneducational organizations include the production of goods and services, the protection of the interests of members, and the provision of some type of help to the organization; and the main purpose of the continuing education agency is to help participants become more proficient in ways that are beneficial to the parent organization, as well as to the individual.

Most agencies in educational and noneducational categories share several characteristics. One characteristic is that the continuing education agency is a dependent unit of an organization whose main purpose is not continuing education of adults. Agencies vary greatly in this regard, from community colleges for which continuing education is a central function to organizations for which continuing education is marginal. A second shared characteristic is that the agency does not have a *faculty*, a group of full-time resource persons, but uses experts on a part-time basis. As a result, program administrators perform many teaching-related roles. Low priority for continuing education and lack of a full-time faculty contribute to the sense of marginality widely noted in continuing education agencies. A third and related characteristic, with several noteworthy exceptions, such as the Cooperative Extension Service, is organizational instability and lack of institutionalization. Fourth is the need to attend to both parent organization and the broader community. Most agencies, even in highly bureaucratic and unresponsive parent organizations, tend to be market oriented, such as business in the private sector. The organizational boundaries of the agency tend to be more permeable and less distinct than in the parent organization and, as a result, people can more easily become participants, resource persons, and administrators than in the parent organization. Internally, as a result of the diverse backgrounds of members and the lack of detailed policies and procedures, organizational control and group cohesiveness tend to be lower in the agency than in the remainder of the parent organization.

The preceding structural characteristics contribute to the desire for greater support from the parent organization that is expressed by some continuing education administrators and the nature of the structure influences strategies to strengthen such support. The dynamics of coordination between agency and parent organization can be analyzed in terms of typical agency-organization relationships.

Agency-Organization Relationships

Satisfactory relationships depend on mutually beneficial exchanges. The following analysis is presented in three sections. These are (1) acquisition of inputs (goals, people, and facilities) by the agency, including influences on that process by the parent organization; (2) planning, conducting, and supporting continuing education activities for adults, including influences by the parent organization; and (3) outcomes of the continuing education agency, including how they relate to the parent organization's purposes and resources (Katz and Kahn, 1978).

Inputs. Agencies vary in the extent to which their own staff handles acquisition of inputs. In very independent agencies (such as the Cooperative Extension Service), all acquisitions are handled by agency staff members within policy and accountability guidelines from the parent organization (land-grant university). In very dependent agencies, (such as a community college in which division directors supervise both preparatory and continuing education), staff members from the parent organization make major decisions about admissions, teaching appointments, fee levels, and typically the agency uses parent organization facilities on a space-available basis.

Attraction of participants is important to all continuing education agencies. Participation is typically voluntary. Educational institutions vary in the selectivity of their admission policies. Consider the contrast between a suburban public school's continuing education division that admits any interested adult and a private university's continuing education division that recruits applicants for evening credit courses but admits fewer than half the applicants.

The determination of agency or client control over admission is central to an agency's responsiveness. For example, private universities' evening credit courses and some company executive development programs depend on the mutuality of admissions requirements and clientele interest, and such programs tend to be responsive and adaptive. By contrast, for mandatory continuing education activities provided by penal institutions for inmates, by school systems for welfare recipients interested in employment, or by the military for recruits, neither the agency nor the clients have much influence on enrollments and admissions. As a result, the agency may face unmotivated participants. In other patterns of admission, the client may elect but the agency must accept, as in the public community college with an open door policy of automatic admission of any high school graduate in the district. More rarely, the client must participate but the agency may reject, as may occur in military education when a program is attractive and important, but budget and placement opportunities restrict enrollments (Houle, 1980).

Parent organizations vary in the extent and type of influence they have on selection of continuing education participants. In earlier years, many agencies had great latitude in decisions about the number and characteristics of their participants. Today, some parent organizations have increased their influence on agency admissions. For example, an employer with targeted human resource development needs will expect the education department to meet specific goals for the number and job titles of the participants. Likewise, a university with declining resident instruction enrollments may increase control over extramural admissions decisions.

One way in which continuing education administrators can strengthen relationships with parent organizations is to work to seek agreement with people in the parent organization who set or influence policies and procedures for recruitment and selection of continuing education participants. For example, supervisors might forecast educational and training needs and set selection criteria for a company, leaders of a professional association might decide selection criteria and procedures for workshops, and a university academic senate might endorse admissions criteria for a special degree program for adults.

Another important input is recruitment and selection of teachers, counselors, writers, and discussion leaders (Brown and Copeland, 1979). Personnel from the parent organization are especially influential in educational organizations. For example, in some school systems union contracts give full-time teachers who have taught adult education courses "first refusal" before the director of adult and continuing education can hire someone from the community. Likewise, in some colleges and universities, department chairs can assign full-time faculty members to teach evening or off-campus credit courses and can decide whether others may do so on an adjunct basis. Administrators in educational parent organizations typically influence the continuing education staffing process by emphasizing compatibility with competing priorities such as research and resident instruction for full-time faculty and qualifications of outsiders who are appointed part time, in order to maintain standards.

Most continuing education administrators come to continuing education positions from previous contact with the parent organization. As they develop associations between their continuing education efforts and those of continuing educators with other types of parent organizations, many develop a secondary allegiance to the broad and emerging field of continuing education. The parent organization does little to advance this secondary allegiance and may even discourage it. It is advanced by reading, collaboration, and participation in professional associations. This participation brings administrators in contact with their counterparts in other types of parent organizations and is especially important because continuing education administrators are the main vehicle for introducing part-time teachers of adults to useful concepts and practices regarding continuing education (Knox and Associates, 1980).

Sometimes program administrators work part time in the agency and part time elsewhere in the parent organization as teachers, counselors, specialists, or administrators. This type of split appointment has advantages and disadvantages. The main advantage is integration of the agency into the parent organization, as occurs when a manager or engineer in a company helps conduct and supervise educational programs or when a faculty member or an associate dean in a higher education institution serves as a part-time program administrator in the continuing education agency. The main disadvantage of split appointments is the fragmentation that tends to occur when so many of those associated with the agency are part time. Split appointments for program administrators and provision of support staff services can be forms of subsidy by the parent organization.

Policies and procedures enable parent organizations to influence the continuing education agency. The person to whom the agency director reports is a major source of guidelines, sometimes formally approved and written, more often informal. Policies may cover decisions regarding participant fees, participant selection criteria, honoraria for resource persons, personnel selection criteria, procedures for approval of new programs, and assignment of charges from one unit of the parent organization to another. Accounting procedures are usually consistent within each parent organization, but continuing education agencies are different enough from other parts of the organization that exceptions are typical.

Finances are a major input, and practices vary within, as well as among, various types of parent organizations. A major consideration is how much of the expenses an agency is expected to recover from income. Some public schools obtain no income from participant fees but pay all expenses from tax funds. By contrast, some private universities recover at least all direct and indirect costs from participant fees. Some employers' education departments charge to participants' budgetary units a prorated share of all educational costs. Other employers allocate funds to an education and training department based on previous performance and current needs, and the department works within those resources. Most religious institutions absorb a major portion of the costs for adult religious education. Professional associations typically seek to recover full costs from participant fees.

When continuing education agencies operate on revolving funds from participant fees, the size of the program can fluctuate with demand, in contrast to programs that are limited by an annual budget allocation. Some parent organizations influence programming by allocating a budget based on anticipated income and then modifying the expense budget as the year proceeds, based on the income.

Facilities, equipment, and supplies are material inputs that are often provided by educational parent organizations. Classrooms, laboratories, instructional equipment, and libraries are often available, especially in the evenings. Agencies typically have their own office space, and sometimes instructional facilities such as extension and conference centers. Agencies in noneducational organizations vary greatly in their arrangements for facilities and equipment. The educational facilities of some employers are among the best in the field. Professional associations usually rent facilities for workshops. Agencies in religious institutions, libraries, and museums use space in the parent organization's facilities. A major consideration is whether unused facilities in the parent organization are available when and where the agency's personnel want to use them. For example, employers typically conduct educational activities during working hours, so their agencies acquire separate facilities. Community colleges typically offer courses in the evening when adults and classrooms are available, so their agencies share facilities. When colleges or schools develop daytime programs for adults, their agencies acquire separate facilities.

Relationships between agencies and their parent organizations reflect organizational demands and constraints. Examples of demands are: meeting human resource development goals for a company or military base, sustaining enrollments of full-time students, or using standard accounting practices. Constraints are limitations on goals and procedures, outside of which the agency can venture only with great risk. Examples of constraints are: curricular standards of educational institutions, cost-recovery guidelines for associations, and topics for patient education in a hospital. Most demands and constraints are not written but are implicit in the functioning of the parent organization. The latitude for most agencies lies between the demands and constraints of the parent organization.

Process. The preceding section identified major inputs of agencies and indicated something of the procedures that are used to acquire them. It also noted variations among agencies, including agency-organization relationships. This section provides an overview of three central processes by which inputs are transformed into outcomes. Relationships between the agency and its parent organization are emphasized. The three processes are program development, finance, and coordination.

Program development includes planning and conducting learning activities. Five major components of this process are needs, setting, objectives, activities, and evaluation. People and traditions from the parent organization can influence each of these components, although over the years continuing education program development has typically been quite independent of the parent organization.

Noneducational organizations have a membership or adult constituency that enables them to contribute to needs assessment. Examples include an employer (such as a hospital) that uses performance review to identify needed educational activities or an association that uses an awareness of policy issues or new practices to select a workshop topic. Educational institutions typically have to reach out to a clientele for purposes of needs assessment.

All parent organizations have purposes and resources that can help set priorities for the continuing education agency. Examples include distinctive faculty members or curricular offerings for educational institutions, and concern about value issues and social problems for religious institutions.

Few parent organizations directly influence the setting of objectives for individual courses and workshops. One exception is use of the same syllabus by educational institutions for evening or off-campus courses and for the resident instructional program. However, after continuing education objectives and activities are offered, administrators and policy makers of the parent organization sometimes have reactions that influence subsequent plans of the agency. This is most evident for controversial topics and for visible successes.

For educational institutions, the subject matter and teaching styles of faculty members who conduct continuing education activities influence both objectives and learning activities. For noneducational organizations, close association with participants as members or constituents produces informal evaluations of the effort. In some settings, such as organizational development activities by employers, the types of information collected during needs assessment are collected again for evaluation purposes (Knox and Associates, 1980). If a parent organization has specialized educational facilities, equipment, and materials for continuing education (for example, a conference center), the agency tends to emphasize activities that are well served by these resources.

One way in which continuing education administrators seek to influence the organization is through advisory and planning committees. For example, a program administrator might include both experts and potential participants, representing both the parent organization and the clientele, on a planning committee designed to produce a continuing education activity likely to have high priority for both the parent organization and the clientele. For educational institutions, faculty involvement in conducting continuing education activities can provide faculty members with examples, materials, visibility, and contacts that benefit other aspects of their faculty roles, such as teaching in the resident instruction program, applied research, or placement of full-time students. Over the years, some program areas begun in continuing education have become part of the resident instruction program. In these ways, continuing education agency activities influence practices in the parent organization.

The flow of funds to and from the agency is a process in which the parent organization usually has some influence. Agencies obtain funds from various sources: tuition and fees paid by participants; financial support by government, employers, foundations, and other sources; and informal subsidy by the parent organization. Organization and agency policies regarding fee levels and financial practices (such as extent of cost recovery and accumulation of venture capital by the agency) influence the acquisition of funds. There are also external influences such as the other continuing education agencies in the service area and their fee levels. The agency uses the resulting funds to acquire resources—staff, participants, physical facilities, and equipment. Sometimes volunteer contributions supplement the resources. Policies and practices of the parent organization influence acquisitions of these inputs, for example, by policies for honorarium and salary guidelines, and charges for facilities. The resulting resources are used in all of the agency's processes, especially the teaching-learning transaction (as reflected in group size and format), which contribute to the agency's outcomes (especially benefits to participants). Influences on the number and characteristics of participants (including sources of financial assistance and competition from other providers) affect the completion of the cycle as potential participants decide whether to enroll as they compare the costs (time, money, effort) with the anticipated benefits.

In addition to the parent organization's influence on agency financial practices, the agency can influence the parent organization. Included are both competition with other parts of the organization for use of funds and facilities, and provision to the organization of resources it would not have otherwise acquired, such as use of facilities during slack periods, employment of underutilized personnel, increased public support, and increased income if agency income exceeds total expenses.

A central concern of most continuing education administrators is coordination. This aspect of administrative leadership is especially important because of the low level of institutionalization that characterizes most agencies. With part-time or short-term participants and resource persons, staff members with little specialized preparation, shared use of facilities, and unpredictability regarding funding, participants, and personnel, continuing education administrators provide a "human cement" that holds many agencies together.

As the agency's administrators seek to relate individual preferences and practices to agency purposes and procedures, there are influences from the service area as well as from the parent organization. Most agency procedures evolved informally with little influence from the parent organization. The effort to avoid problems or seek opportunities means formal policies tend to be established after the practices evolve. Policy boards of parent organizations have given little attention to continuing education until recent years when in educational institutions it was seen as a way to compensate for declining enrollments of full-time students.

Administrators seek to establish policies and procedures that will help achieve consensus on agency objectives and coordinate contributions to the achievement of those objectives. Policies and procedures are most effective when they are internalized by people associated with the agency. Some administrators have set up advisory committees composed of various combinations of personnel from the parent organization and representatives from the clientele to help with formulation and implementation of policies. One attractive feature of continuing education has been its contribution to the growing edge of the parent organization. Increased formalization of policy and procedures can injure that venturesomeness.

Outcomes. The primary outcome of continuing education is enhanced proficiency of participants. Adults apply what they learn in their roles in family, work, and community, which in turn benefits society. Some participants may use their contact with the agency for extraeducational benefits, as when attendance or a certificate (regardless of enhanced proficiency) satisfies requirements for job entry or relicensure.

There are also secondary outcomes for the parent organization, but their value usually depends on the benefit of primary outcomes. For example, continuing education is good public relations for the parent organization only if it is effective, otherwise it harms public relations. A secondary outcome is the impact on community organizations and on other continuing education providers. Other secondary outcomes relate mainly to the parent organization and include level of general understanding and support of the parent organization, increased use of personnel and facilities, and increased organizational effectiveness. For educational organizations, increased organizational effectiveness results when faculty members gain examples and materials to be used in the preparatory education program. For noneducational organizations, increased organizational effectiveness results from members' improved performance.

Leadership

Studies of continuing education agencies have found that administrators can make a major difference regarding the vitality and effectiveness of an agency (Knox, 1980; Mezirow, Darkenwald, and Knox, 1975). Effective administrators understand the agency as a social system, relating it to both parent organization and service area. Related proficiencies include a perspective in the field that enables the administrator to refer program ideas and requests for programs to other agencies when they are better suited to respond and to identify emerging issues early enough to respond to attractive opportunities in a timely way (Knox, 1979a). Effective administrators also recognize the importance of sound program development procedures that take into account the interests of both the clientele and the parent organization.

This concern is reflected in the inclusion of both viewpoints in needs-assessment and evaluation activities. Another indication of effective administration is the use of multiple sources and incentives to acquire major inputs. Examples include multiple sources of financial support and multiple incentives in marketing activities to attract participants and resource persons.

Continuing education agencies are complex systems and, as such, their functioning depends on the quality of each component and on articulation among components. Agency leadership includes attention not only to internal functioning, but also to external relationships, and a relationship with the parent organization is an important part of those external relationships. An awareness of how administrators of other types of continuing education agencies seek to strengthen organizational relationships can enable administrators to better understand their own agencies.

References

Brown, M. A., and Copeland, H. (Eds.). *New Directions for Continuing Education: Attracting Able Instructors of Adults*, no 4. San Francisco: Jossey-Bass, 1979.

Houle, C. O. *Continuing Learning in the Professions.* San Francisco: Jossey-Bass, 1980.

Katz, D., and Kahn, R. L. *The Social Psychology of Organizations.* (2nd ed.) New York: Wiley, 1978.

Knox, A. B. (Ed.). *New Directions for Continuing Education: Enhancing Proficiencies of Continuing Educators*, no. 1. San Francisco: Jossey-Bass, 1979a.

Knox, A. B. (Ed.). *New Directions for Continuing Education: Assessing the Impact of Continuing Education*, no. 3. San Francisco: Jossey-Bass, 1979b.

Knox, A. B. *University Continuing Professional Education: Organizational Dynamics in Medicine, Pharmacy, Social Work, Education, and Law.* Urbana: University of Illinois, 1980.

Knox, A. B., and Associates. *Developing, Administering, and Evaluating Adult Education.* San Francisco: Jossey-Bass, 1980.

Mezirow, J., Darkenwald, G., and Knox, A. B. *Last Gamble on Education.* Washington, D.C.: Adult Education Association of the U.S.A., 1975.

Alan B. Knox is professor of continuing education at the University of Illinois at Urbana-Champaign. He has broad experience in continuing education of adults as a teacher, administrator, professor, researcher, writer, and consultant.

Strengthening organizational support for continuing education requires continuing educators who are proficient at designing and managing the organizational change process.

Strategies for Organizational Change

James C. Votruba

Strengthening organizational support for continuing education occurs through the process of planned organizational adaptation and change. In this sense, continuing educators who hope to enlarge organizational support for continuing education must focus their efforts not only on identifying those organizational changes that need to occur, but also on the development of a well-designed and well-managed strategy for accomplishing them. Accordingly, this chapter examines the planned change process in complex organizations with particular emphasis upon the role of the continuing educator as change agent.

Conceptualizing Change

A strategy for strengthening organizational support for continuing education should reflect an appropriate conceptual view of the organizational change process. Building upon the pioneer work of Havelock and his associates at the University of Michigan's Center for Research on the Utilization of Scientific Knowledge, Lindquist (1978) suggests that there are essentially four different sets of assumptions concerning what leads people or organizations to change. These four sets of assumptions are represented by four very different conceptual approaches to planned change. Lindquist names these approaches Rational Planning (research, development, diffusion), Social Interaction, Human Problem Solving, and

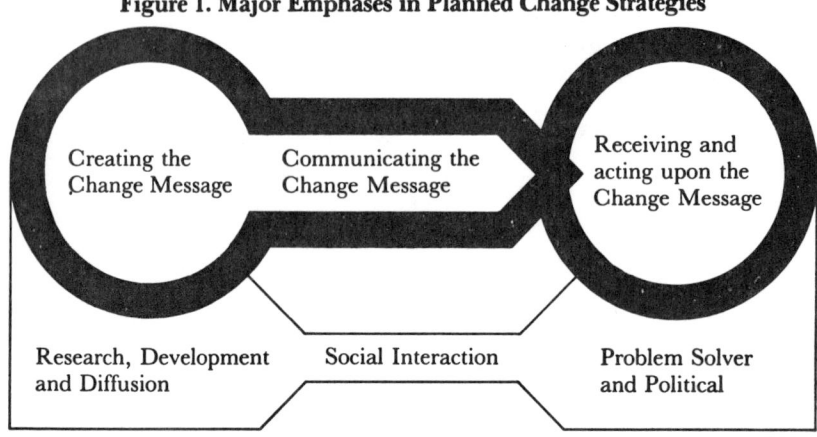

Figure 1. Major Emphases in Planned Change Strategies

Source: Lindquist, 1978.

Political. He suggests that each can be viewed as emphasizing a different aspect of the basic communication act.

Rational Planning. The rational planning approach assumes that change occurs on the basis of reason and evidence. Accordingly, the best way to create change in an organization is through systematic research and development of new knowledge, new practices, and new products. If the research is correct and the development sound, the proposed change will sell itself. The emphasis is on creating the strongest possible message for the desired change. Guba (1968) and Clark and Guba (1965) found this approach often used in the development and diffusion of educational innovation. This same approach is also found in the research, development, and diffusion efforts of the corporate sector.

The rational planning approach can be seen at work in educational organizations through the encouragement of committees and task forces to study a particular problem and formulate a solution based upon the best evidence available. For example, a college president might convene a task force to study how the campus can strengthen support for its continuing education mission. The task force would research the problem, consider alternatives, and recommend a solution. The president, along with other decision makers, would then study the recommendations and decide whether they were appropriate. Given their perceived appropriateness, the president might then communicate the recommendations to the deans for implementation.

The problem with this approach is that organizations, like the individuals and groups within them, do not function simply as rational systems, thoughtfully accepting the latest innovations. In addition, what may be logical to one person may not be logical to another. Lindquist (1978) suggests that a major shortcoming of the rational planning approach is the frequent isolation of the planners from the people who will ultimately be responsible for and affected by the proposed change. There is no doubt that reason and evidence are vital ingredients in the organizational change process; however, an effective change strategy must include more than compelling logic. Adoption of a proposed organizational change may depend as much on how the change message is communicated as it does upon the strength of the change message itself.

Social Interaction. Social networks are an important part of any organization. They provide individuals and groups with security, status, and esteem as well as offering interpretations regarding activity within the organization. Everett Rogers (Rogers, Agarivala-Rogers, and Lee, 1975; Rogers and Shoemaker, 1971) is characteristic of researchers who maintain that these social networks are essential to organizational change. For the social interactionists, the process of communicating the change message is as important as the message itself.

Identifying and utilizing opinion leaders within the organization is an important element in the social interaction approach to change. The most persuasive communicator usually has the expertise, experience, or social role to be perceived as a credible source of the information presented (Rosnow and Robinson, 1967). Those who wish to strengthen organizational support for continuing education must enlist the support and involvement of these opinion leaders. For example, a college continuing education dean may produce a compelling rationale for increased faculty rewards for conducting continuing education but the case will be more persuasive if several key faculty members and academic administrators join in communicating that message to the campus.

Lindquist (1978) points out that social interaction researchers identify certain attributes of innovation (in addition to impressive reason and evidence) that influence eventual adoption. For example, does the innovative have clear relative advantages for the individual, group, or organization? Is the innovation compatible with dominant values and traditions? Is the innovation divisible so that it can be adopted a bit at a time? Is it simple to understand and accomplish? Does it involve low risk and low uncertainty? Can it be tried and observed before making an irrevocable commitment? These are questions that should be addressed when designing communication of the change message.

Human Problem Solving. While rational planning and social interaction are important elements in the planned change process, many researchers suggest that the most important elements are rooted in the psychological dimension of change (Argyris and Schön, 1974; Parsons, 1974; Watson, 1972). For these researchers, such underlying psychological factors as fear, anxiety, prejudice, need for dependence or independence, and need for autonomy have the greatest influence on attitudes towards change. Unless uncovered and dealt with, these factors thwart attempts to change an organization. To the extent that the organizational climate lacks trust and openness, these psychological factors will tend to be extremely difficult to uncover and may take on even greater significance. For example, if a proposed change raises considerable fear and anxiety among those who will be most affected by it, all the logic and rationality in the world will be insufficient to gain its acceptance.

For those who advocate this approach to planned change, it is vitally important that the change strategy be based on a clear understanding of the psychological forces that will influence acceptance or rejection. For example, several years ago a Midwestern university developed a comprehensive plan to strengthen and expand its lifelong education mission. The plan was well developed and consistent with the university's land-grant charter. Nevertheless, the plan met with intensive faculty opposition which resulted in much of it being either abandoned or modified. Later analysis of the resistance revealed that it had nothing to do with opposition to lifelong education per se. Indeed, most faculty members supported campus lifelong education activities. Rather, faculty opposition arose out of considerable anxiety over their job security and the fear that such a huge commitment to lifelong education would drain already scarce resources from their colleges and departments. In addition, many feared that they would be forced to engage in teaching and service activities for which they had neither the time nor the interest. If these deep-rooted sources of resistance had been discovered early and incorporated into the planned change strategy, the outcome might have been much different.

The Human Problem Solving approach places special importance upon creating a psychologically supportive environment for change and making the change responsive to the needs of the users. Collaboration, openness, consensus, trust, self-initiation, and ownership are important elements in this approach and need to be considered when designing a change strategy. Outside consultants are frequently used to gain better understanding of the user's world and to discover and address sources of organizational resistance to planned change. The problem with this approach is that it can be terrifically time consuming and expensive and still fail (Zaltman and Duncan, 1977).

Political. The Rational Planning approach to change emphasizes developing and arguing an impressive case. The Social Interaction approach takes that case, puts it in terms attractive to its audience, and then introduces it through opinion leaders to their various reference groups. The Human Problem Solving approach attempts to break down resistance to change by making the change responsive to the needs of the users. Finally, the Political approach offers yet another perspective by focusing upon the political process that depicts the course of planned change in political systems (Easton, 1965).

Baldridge (1971) suggests that a simple political model begins with the social conditions that promote the formation of divergent views and interest groups. For example, lack of agreement could occur over the issue of whether an organization should further develop continuing education. The next step involves interest articulation. How do the interest groups influence the decision-making process? This step frequently involves identifying and influencing gatekeepers who can get the proposed change on the decision maker's agenda and keep it there until acted upon. Interest articulation leads to legislative transformation, which results in an official organizational policy. Finally, the policy is formally executed, which provides feedback to the original interest groups who in turn must decide whether further action is required.

The Political approach to planned organizational change emphasizes power, influence, and leverage. Primary importance is placed upon building coalitions, identifying and influencing gatekeepers, designing compromises, and using leverage based upon political advantage. The weakness of the approach is that much can be done by individuals and groups within the organization to ensure that an unpopular policy is never implemented in any significant way.

Combining Approaches. Lindquist (1978, p. 9) suggests that the strongest approach to planned organizational change is through a synthesis of the preceding approaches in which the strengths of each are employed. He writes:

> Is it not possible to entertain the notion that humans are rational social creatures who want to solve their hidden problems but also want to protect and enhance their vested interests? If we make such an assumption, we must combine our strategies for change. Rational research and planning is not enough. Nor is connecting innovations to opinion leaders in all the right ways. Nor is skilled intervention to diagnose human needs and to reduce resistance. Nor is the most effective political maneuvering. We must do it all.

Havelock and others (1969) use the concept of *linkage* to develop a general change model that combines the several approaches to change discussed above. They suggest that planned change begins with a felt need on the part of the person, group, or organization which might change. Something is wrong. Some improvement is needed. For example, a university continuing education agency is having difficulty recruiting and retaining faculty members to conduct their continuing education programs. This problem is affecting the general growth and vitality of the campus outreach program.

The next step is diagnosis of the problem. In our example, the continuing education staff gets together and tries to assess why they are not able to effectively recruit and retain faculty members. They consult with local faculty members and academic administrators for an assessment of the problem as well as for possible solutions. Identification of alternative courses of action follows. Raise faculty pay for continuing education involvement. Develop a more effective faculty orientation program. Strengthen support from leaders around the campus. Expand the criteria for faculty promotion and tenure to include continuing education involvement as well as traditional scholarship and teaching.

Finally, a solution for the specific problem is developed and implementation follows. Often this implementation raises other needs, and the problem-solving cycle begins again.

Meanwhile, outside the local setting, there is an external resource system of persons and organizations who are familiar with the problem and can assist in addressing it.

Figure 2 summarizes the Havelock linkage model. Of special significance is the linking of those experiencing the particular problem with the external resource system that can assist in its resolution. The continuing education agency which is having difficulty recruiting and retaining faculty needs to be linked with individuals or organizations which have experienced the same problem. This can be done in various ways. Use of consultants is one approach. Development of networks that link people with similar problems is another approach.

The point is that the Havelock model describes an interactive process that links those with the problem to those who can assist in the solution. Lindquist (1978) suggests that this particular approach to planned change is useful in that it provides the opportunity to integrate the breadth of experience and background of the resource system with the particular situation of the client (user) system.

The Havelock model contributes to an understanding of how organizations change. However, one of its limitations, particularly for administrators, is its abstractness. Writing about planned change in collegiate settings, Lindquist uses the Havelock model to develop his own adaptive development model of planned change in colleges and universities. Summarized in Figure 3, the Lindquist (1978) approach is more specific and concrete in describing the process of organizational change and has application in a wide variety of collegiate and other organizations. By combining the strengths of the various approaches to planned change previously described, the Lindquist model provides considerable insight for continuing educators who wish to design a process for strengthening organizational support for continuing education.

Designing for Change Strategies

The preceding discussion of conceptual approaches contains several important factors to help continuing educators design a planned change

Figure 2. A Linkage View of Resource-User Problem-Solving

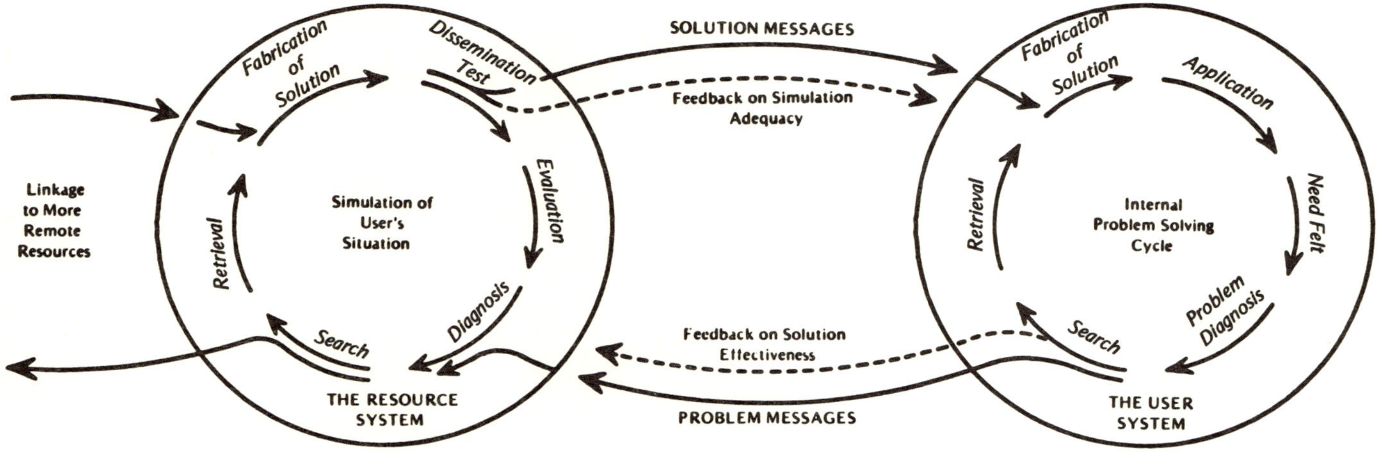

Source: Havelock, 1973.

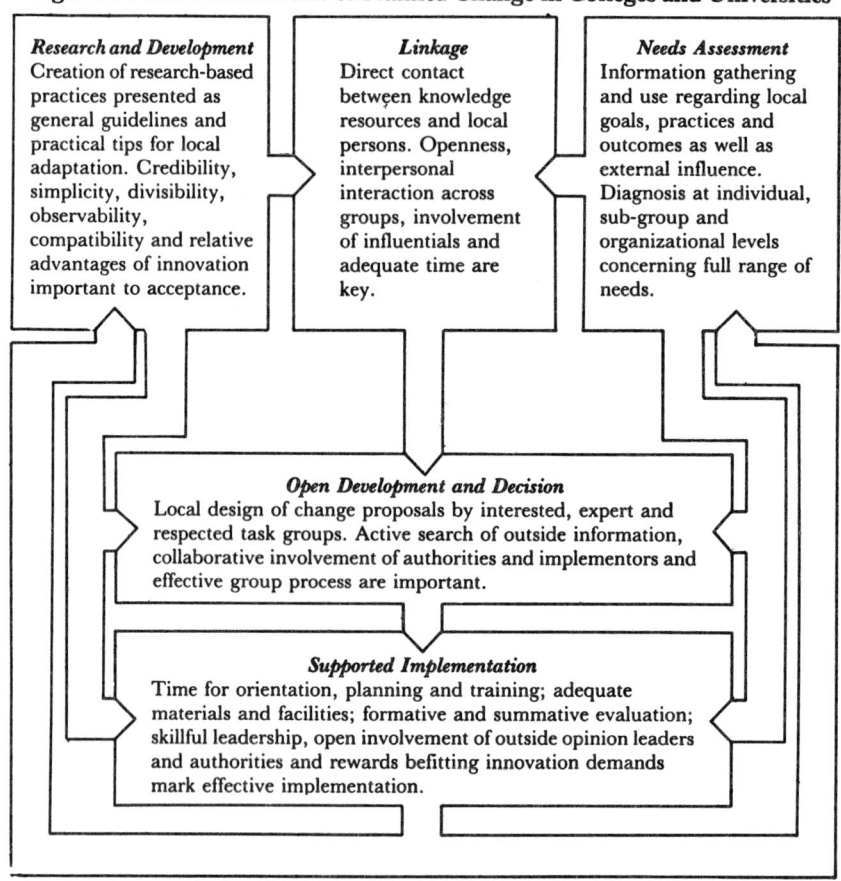

Figure 3. Process and Factors of Planned Change in Colleges and Universities

Source: Lindquist, 1978.

strategy. When change strategies fail in their objectives, it is often because one or more of these factors have not received enough thoughtful attention. The most important of these factors are described below.

Goals. The design of strategies should evolve from a clear and precise understanding of the goals of the planned change process. What is to be accomplished? What are the intended outcomes? In this regard, it is not enough to simply want to strengthen organizational support for continuing education. This general goal needs to be divided into specific subgoals around which planned change strategies can be developed. For example, strengthening support within a public school setting might involve increasing the marketing effort, educating policy makers, orienting teachers, or opening a satellite center. Planned change strategies can be designed to address each of these goals. Without a precise understanding of what is to be accomplished, strategies often lack direction and continuity.

Organization. Planned change strategies are more apt to succeed if they are systematically organized and coordinated. While this may seem obvious, it is remarkable how many fail because they are conceived or implemented in a haphazard fashion. The result is that problems often are not properly analyzed and defined, the most appropriate solutions are not thoroughly examined, available resources are not used, sources of organizational support and resistance are not identified, or ideas are introduced at the wrong time. There is no doubt that thorough organization is a key to successful planned change. The planned change effort that moves too rapidly, involves too few people, and lacks sufficient information is apt to encounter serious problems (Kotter and Schlesinger, 1979).

Leadership. An important aspect of a successful change strategy is the presence of strong leadership in support of the change effort. Lindquist (1978) suggests that effective leadership for planned change includes a combination of initiating change activities, structuring, guiding, pushing, supporting the planned change process, linking people with ideas, and involving both the influentials and the implementors in the entire process. Those designing a planned change strategy must examine sources of potential leadership both within their own continuing education agency and within the larger parent organization. Who are the potential leaders? What steps can be taken to involve them in the planned change process? Leadership for strengthening organizational support for continuing education should, whenever possible, involve not only continuing educators but also influential people from the parent organization. Indeed, organizational change is rarely successful unless it enjoys considerable support from top organizational management (Lawrence and Lorsch, 1969).

Linkage. Another factor associated with successful planned change is connecting the people responsible for and affected by the intended change with resources that can be used to support the change effort.

Linkage that supports the intended change can take many forms. It can involve linking organizational decision makers with their counterparts in other institutions where the change has already occurred. It can involve linking those people working for the change with potential sources of financial support. It often involves linking supporters of the intended change with new knowledge and perspectives that will strengthen their ability to be advocates for the change. It should also include educating those people who are giving direction to the change process with the dynamics of planned change in complex organizations.

Effective linkage in support of planned change requires a thorough familiarity with both the organization in which the change is to occur and the internal and external resource system that can support the change effort.

Openness. Another factor to be considered when designing a strategy is how best to create an environment in which the intended change will be considered with openness and honesty. This is particularly important in two respects. First, it is essential that those people who are involved in accomplishing the intended change feel free to express their ideas, doubts, and concerns throughout the formulation and implementation of the strategy. Without this candor, many valuable insights and warnings may be overlooked. Second, it is vitally important that opponents of the intended change also have the opportunity to express their objections openly and honestly. It is more difficult to deal with the opposition if they are an unknown element. In framing a strategy for strengthening organizational support for continuing education, leaders should pay close attention to creating a supportive environment and an opportunity for both supporters and opponents to speak their minds freely.

Capacity. Another important consideration when designing a planned change strategy is to ensure that the material and human resources involved in the effort are sufficient. For example, are there adequate financial resources? Do those who are primarily responsible for implementing the strategy possess the needed expertise and commitment? Should others be included in either design or implementation because of their particular expertise or influence? Continuing educators who wish to strengthen organizational support for continuing education need to evaluate what is needed to accomplish their particular objectives and then identify the human and material resources required for the task. This assessment may often lead to reducing the initial objectives to fit available resources. The key is to not attempt more than you have the resources to support.

Compatibility. Designers and managers of organizational change strategies should strive for compatibility between the intended change and the values, traditions, priorities, and needs of the organization in which the change must occur. Gaining acceptance of change is enhanced to the extent that it is perceived to support that which is most central and most important to the organization. For example, a Midwest land-grant university recently strengthened faculty support for a new off-campus, adult-oriented liberal studies program by demonstrating that all of the program components (independent study, off-campus instruction, interdisciplinary seminars), were currently being practiced somewhere in the university. This program would simply bring them together in a unique way. In addition, the program was described as consistent with the service emphasis of the land-grant tradition and likely to be viewed by state government officials as evidence of the university's commitment to meeting the educational needs of the state. In this way it contributed to strengthened political support.

Even the most exciting and progressive innovation stands little chance of acceptance if it is incompatible with the organization itself. In this regard, continuing educators who wish to strengthen organizational support for continuing education need to demonstrate how the innovation will enhance those values, traditions, priorities, and needs which are most important to the organization.

Rewards. People as well as organizations relinquish old attitudes or behaviors and adopt new ones because of some incentive for them to do so. When designing planned change strategies, it is important to identify those people upon whom the change depends and to analyze the rewards and incentives that currently exist or could be developed to motivate their support. These rewards may be intrinsic (satisfaction, status, enjoyment, prestige), or extrinsic (money, academic rank) and may exist at the individual, group, or organizational level (Votruba, 1979). For example, a new off-campus degree program for adults might provide involved faculty members with increased income, greater visibility and status among practitioners in the field, greater opportunity for consulting with state agencies, or the enjoyment of working with adults. The same program might also provide the department chairperson and college dean with a larger number of instructional units which are used to measure academic productivity and acquire campus financial support. The program might further appeal to campus policy makers because of its potential for increasing statewide visibility and thereby building state political support. A major element of any planned change strategy should be to identify those individuals and groups within the organization upon whom acceptance of the change depends and to analyze the incentives which may influence their support or opposition.

Rewards are also important for those who are most directly involved in trying to accomplish the change. Planned change in organizations can be a long, lonely, difficult, frustrating process. While the ultimate incentive may be accomplishing the change itself, it is important that there be more immediate and incremental rewards and incentives along the way. For example, it is helpful if those working for the change enjoy each other and enjoy getting together and working as a team. It is also important for those involved to celebrate the little successes along the way. Leaders should be quick to recognize significant contributions to the change effort and give credit for jobs well done. Leaders should also keep in mind that those who are working to accomplish the change are generally provided additional incentive by being able to satisfy some of their own personal goals and needs while at the same time working toward the goals of the change process.

Synergy. For those who hope to strengthen organizational support for continuing education, synergy refers to the number, variety, strength, and frequency of forces that can be combined to support the planned change. These forces may be either internal or external to the organization. They may include individuals or groups who have the capacity to influence the organization or its decision makers. They may also include demographic, social, economic, and political trends to which the organization is sensitive.

For example, assume that the goal is to expand a university's involvement in continuing professional educaton. Support for such an effort might be found among certain campus deans, department heads, senior faculty members, and administrators. Support might also exist among various professional associations, public policy makers, corporate executives, and alumni. In addition, campus enrollments may be dropping because of demographic shifts; political trends may be producing greater pressure for the university to demonstrate its service commitment; and trends in technological development may be forcing some professionals to constantly update. All of these forces might be used to make the case for expanded programming in continuing professional education.

Those responsible for guiding the change process need to recognize the full range of external and internal forces that can be used to support the planned change effort. They must then carefully select those forces that, when combined, create the desired effect. This process requires insight into the organization itself and the environment in which it functions.

Ownership. A major consideration when designing a planned change strategy should be the extent to which those upon whom the change depends feel that they have a part in its development. Strengthening organizational support for continuing education will generally require the understanding, acceptance, time, and skills of various individuals and groups throughout the organization. These people need to be involved in the earliest stages of the change process and to stay involved throughout. They must be encouraged to invest enough of themselves in the process to have a stake in the outcome. They must see the project as theirs and not simply someone else's. If this sense of ownership can be established and maintained, the change process has a better chance of success.

Designing a change strategy is no easy task, but the considerations described above can be helpful. It is important to remember that a strategy is only a means to an end and not an end in itself. Once an initial strategy has been developed for a particular change objective, that strategy should be frequently reviewed in order to judge its appropriateness in light of new knowledge or changing circumstances. Those responsible for guiding the change process need to take time for periodic reevaluation. Like organizations themselves, change strategies need to be adaptive to remain relevant.

Managing Change

This chapter has thus far examined several conceptual approaches to the organizational change process and analyzed some key factors to consider when designing a change strategy. Several important considerations in managing the planned change process will now be discussed.

Planned Change Team. The formulation and implementation of an organizational change strategy often can be facilitated by bringing together several supporters of the intended change and forming a planned change team (French and Bell, 1973; Lindquist, 1979; Miles, 1959; Reilly and Jones, 1974). This team can help design and manage each step of the problem-solving process, including defining the problem; clarifying the change objectives; searching out and retrieving relevant information; formulating appropriate strategies; gaining individual, group, and organizational acceptance and support; implementing the change; and evaluating the outcomes.

Introducing change in complex organizations is often a difficult, complex, and discouraging process. Organizing the change effort around a small team of individuals can offer several important advantages. First, the change team has the potential for generating greater energy, influence, and expertise than a single person working alone. Second, the team allows for a division of labor based upon interests and competencies. For example, it would be extraordinarily difficult for a single person to attend to all the factors mentioned above as important considerations in any change strategy. The team can divide the factors and ensure that none is overlooked. Third, team members can assist each other when the going gets tough, as it often does at some point during the process. Finally, the team activity can become personally beneficial as a learning and social experience.

Lindquist (1979) suggests that the composition of a team will have a critical influence upon its effectiveness. In this regard, he offers four factors to consider when creating a change team. Do the team members have credibility with each other and with those in the organization upon whom the change depends? Are team members interested in the problem being considered? If a team member has considerable credibility but lacks interest, the contribution is likely to be minimal. Do the team members have the time to devote to the problem-solving process? This is a frequent obstacle in planned change efforts because those persons who enjoy high organizational credibility—even if they have the interest—may not have the time to devote. Do the team members collectively have the expertise needed to address the problem? This expertise should include not only a considerable understanding of the problem itself but also an understanding of the planned change process.

Continuing educators who are trying to deepen organizational commitment to continuing education often make the mistake of coming down too heavily upon the organizational credibility of team members and neglecting the other three characteristics. There is no doubt that credibility is important, particularly when the change process involves strengthening support for a function that may not be central to the organization's primary mission. However, in order for a team to be effective, its members must also have the interest, time, and expertise to address the problem.

Leadership. When planned organizational change is successful, it is generally because the change process has had the benefit of strong, articulate, and adaptive leadership. In this regard, continuing educators who intend to assume leadership for change should possess the following characteristics. They should have a sharp understanding of the organization in which the change is to take place, its values, traditions, and priorities. They should be able to identify opinion leaders and know where, how, and when ideas should be introduced in order to receive appropriate consideration. They should understand the human and material resources needed for the planned change effort and how to marshal resources to support the effort. They should have a keen understanding of their own strengths and weaknesses and be able to recruit team members and other supporters who complement themselves as well as each other. They should understand the planned change process in complex organizations and be able to maintain a total system view of change and its effects. They should be able to anticipate the effect of a particular change on other organizational subsystems as well as on other sectors of the external community. They should closely monitor the organization's external environment for new conditions that may enhance or inhibit the planned change effort. For example, these conditions may include demographic shifts and trends, new state and federal legislation, technological breakthroughs, and changing economic conditions. They should understand their leadership function and be able to adapt their style to suit the circumstances while progressing through the planned change process.

Havelock (1973) suggests that there are four major leadership roles that can be played in the process of change. Depending upon the circumstances, the style of leadership required may shift throughout the change process.

The catalyst is often needed to get things going. They serve to overcome inertia and prod the organization into acknowledging the problem and devoting some time and resources to its resolution. In this sense, the catalyst challenges the status quo and energizes the problem-solving process. From time to time the change leader may be called upon to play this catalytic role throughout the change effort. Spirits may need to be lifted or challenges, reemphasized. The organization may have to be reminded of the urgency of the problem.

A second leadership role is that of solution giver, or authority. In this context, the change leader may be prompted to play the expert, to give answers, to choose among alternatives, or to design the change strategy. There is no doubt that the role of solution giver is periodically important in contributing to both the effectiveness as well as the efficiency of the change process. However, if leaders are too pronounced in their solution-giver role, they run the risk of appearing to dominate the process and others will never develop a sense of involvement and ownership. The key is to know when and how to function as the solution giver.

A third leadership role is that of process helper. Frequently, those involved in trying to accomplish a particular organizational change have a clear sense of their goal but are not sure how to move toward it. They lack a clear understanding of the planned change process. The change leader can offer suggestions regarding such issues as how to define the problem, how to assess alternative approaches, how to build support, and how to design and manage a change strategy, and thus help to establish continuity and direction for the planned change process.

A fourth leadership role is that of the resource linker. Here the leader is called upon to match needs with resources. The planned change process may require such resources as additional information, expertise, financial support, staff, and outside perspective. These resources may exist within or outside the organization. The role of the resource linker is to identify the needs, locate the resources to meet those needs, and link the two together. This leadership function is no doubt a key to effective planned change strategies.

It is unusual for a planned change leader to be able to play all of these roles with equal effectiveness. What is important is that the leader recognize the various functions required throughout the change process and recruit others to assist in the leadership effort.

Vision and Beyond

Strengthening organizational support for continuing education requires both a clear vision of those changes that need to occur and a well-designed and well-managed strategy for accomplishing them. Accordingly, this chapter has briefly looked at several conceptual approaches to organizational change, examined factors essential to designing a planned change strategy, and highlighted some important considerations in managing the planned change effort.

Strengthening organizational support for continuing education may often be difficult and complex but, as the following chapters suggest, it is certainly possible. The chances of success are much higher when continuing educators possess a broad understanding of the organizational change process. This chapter has attempted to enhance such understanding.

References

Argyris, C., and Schön, D. A. *Theory in Practice: Increasing Professional Effectiveness.* San Francisco: Jossey-Bass, 1974.

Baldridge, J. V. *Power and Conflict in the University*. New York: Wiley, 1971.

Clark, D., and Guba, E. "An Examination of Potential Change Roles in Education." Paper presented at Symposium on Innovation in Planning School Curricula, Airlie House, Va., October 1965.

Easton, D. *A Systems Analysis of Political Life*. New York: Wiley, 1965.

French, W., and Bell, C. *Organization Development*. Englewood Cliffs, N.J.: Prentice-Hall, 1973.

Guba, E. "Development, Diffusion, and Evaluation." In T. L. Eidell and J. M. Kitchel (Eds.), *Knowledge Production and Utilization in Educational Administration*. Eugene, Ore.: University Council on Educational Administration and Center for Advanced Study of Educational Administration, 1968.

Havelock, R. G., and others. *Planning for Innovation Through the Dissemination* wood Cliffs, N.J.: Educational Technology Publications, 1973.

Havelock, R. G., and others: *Planning for Innovation Through the Dissemination and Utilization of Knowledge*. Ann Arbor, Mich.: Institute for Social Research, 1969.

Kotter, J., and Schlesinger, L. "Choosing Strategies for Change." *Harvard Business Review*, 1979, *57* (2), 106–114.

Lawrence, P., and Lorsch, J. *Developing Organizations: Diagnosis and Action*. Reading, Mass.: Addison-Wesley, 1969.

Lindquist, J. *Strategies for Change*. Washington, D.C.: Council for the Advancement of Small Colleges (CASC), 1978.

Lindquist, J. *Team Building for Innovation*. Sourcebook for Adult Learning and Planned Change. Memphis, Tenn.: Institute for Academic Improvement, Memphis State University, 1979.

Miles, M. *Learning to Work in Groups: A Guide for Educational Leaders*. New York: Teachers College Press, Columbia University, 1959.

Parsons, T. "Stability and Change in the American University." *Daedalus*, 1974, *103*, 271.

Reilly, A., and Jones, J. "Team Building." In *1974 Annual Handbook for Group Facilitations*. San Diego: University Associates, 1974.

Rogers, M. E., Agarivala-Rogers, R., and Lee, C. C. *Diffusion of IMPACT Innovations to University Professors*. New York: Exxon Foundation, 1975.

Rogers, M. E., and Shoemaker, F. F. *Communication of Innovation*. New York: Free Press, 1971.

Rosnow, R., and Robinson, E. *Experiments in Persuasion*. New York: Academic Press, 1967.

Votruba, J. C. "Developing a Comprehensive Reward System." In M. A. Brown and H. G. Copeland (Eds.), *New Directions for Continuing Education: Attracting Able Instructors of Adults*, no. 4. San Francisco: Jossey-Bass, 1979.

Watson, G. "Resistance to Change." In G. Zaltman, P. Kotter, and I. Kaufman (Eds.), *Creating Social Change*. New York: Holt, Rinehart and Winston, 1972.

Zaltman, G., and Duncan, R. *Strategies for Planned Change*. New York: Wiley, 1977.

James C. Votruba is associate director of the Office of Continuing Education and Public Service and assistant professor of both continuing education and higher education at the University of Illinois at Urbana-Champaign.

*Strategies to enhance the spirit of colleagueship with
other campus groups will ultimately determine how
well continuing education leaders influence
institutional mission and organization.*

Strengthening the University Continuing Education Mission

Paul A. Miller

"Tired students; tired teachers; tired books!" This exclamation was made at a faculty conference held to enlarge awareness of evening courses in continuing education—uttered by a full professor and noted teacher-scholar of the parent university. It was his way of making clear that no amount of persuasion or incentive would encourage him to participate in continuing education efforts. Small wonder, then, that the local director of continuing education would feel the rise of an already high level of paranoia, and that he vented it at the next convention of fellow directors.

Indeed, despite the modern coming of age of continuing education —its remarkable growth and acceptance in educational institutions, in governments, and in the society-at-large—leaders of the field continue to press for, and write about, organizational support for continuing education. Surely one of the recurrent and remarkable episodes in educational history is the valiant struggle by continuing educators to have their field accepted on par with others in their parent organization.

Nevertheless, along with the quantitative and qualitative advance of continuing education, directors need to be aggressive and always on guard, lest the gains now being won will be eroded even more quickly than they were achieved. To improve communication and strengthen cooperation, and to stabilize and enhance what has already been achieved (especially with respect to academic institutions) calls for organizational interventions, which are unlikely to occur without the creative attention of continuing educators themselves.

Throughout more than 800 years, and contrary to frequent myth, even the earliest colleges and universities were shaped by social needs and pressures (Reeves, 1969). Moreover, they have never been free of accountability—whether to king or lord, the papacy, court (as in Scotland), or to the city councils (as in the great wave of European civic universities). However, for that same long history, academic institutions reluctantly accepted, made legitimate, and developed those programs at the nexus of university and society which require a cooperative sponsorship. The absence of the faculties at the coronations of early general extension models and the worried reluctance of the land-grant universities from 1909 to 1914 to find room for cooperative extension (as Seaman A. Knapp promoted his new idea outside them) serve as examples of the curious paradox of American universities. Historically, schools have been uplifted by public need and interest but do not follow through with vigorous and sustained outreach.

What may be said about such a paradox? What confusions, if not conflicts, underlie its historic presence in university development?

Continuing education, which to exist must function at the intersection of contemporary and community needs, has found it difficult to enter, feel at home with, and be fully accepted in the collegial doctrine that has come down to modern institutions through the centuries (Farmer and Knox, 1977). The blurred, overlapping, and sometimes conflicting forms of academic governance are especially disconcerting to the identity of continuing education as a function and continuing educators as professional practitioners. Thus, continuing education, facing students whose learning may be a continuing rather than a singularly paramount, short-term activity, must be aligned with administrative-legal and professional styles of governance, even as it keeps a foothold in the collegial model (Baldridge and others, 1978). Meanwhile, traditional faculty do not see in the adult part-time student the master-apprentice relationships which the collegial model has actively sustained. Continuing education may pay the price of less than full acceptance at the center of collegial tradition which, in the end, influences (perhaps properly) the conduct of most universities.

This blurring of identity is further reinforced by the wide variations in organizational style of continuing education within universities. From distinct and separate faculties and colleges to highly dispersed and overlapping organizational modes, continuing education, contrasted with most academic functions, presents no customary, standard, or expected organizational posture. Similarly, the wide dispersion of continuing education providers beyond the university campus, and the greatly varied definitions of role, function, and organization which they develop, serves only to confuse further the perceptions of identity within the traditional academic sector.

However, whatever the organization, continuing education as part of the university structure carries with it a major identity with professional education. The long-term willingness of universities to assign to separate schools of education the responsibilities for pedagogical philosophy, theory, and methodology has not only weakened the capability of the whole universty in pedagogical practice, it has also accorded lesser status to those who do. This diminishes the identity that continuing education partly shares. And despite the breadth of subject matter and substantive links of continuing educators, their own preparation, self-conceptions, and professional associations tend to an acceptance of such a position in the academic status hierarchy. While less clear, the recruitment of continuing education directors seems also to follow such constricted practice.

Finally, a certain pragmatism commonly informs the perception of need for continuing education by both the faculties and administrators of the parent university. "The students are less than serious." "Their motives are born of crisis or occupational goals, rather than of a desire for genuine learning." "Continuing education is a public service, important, even necessary, but of less significance than full-time traditional missions." "If it is community service, let the community pay for continuing education; if it is not a community service, but classroom instruction, let the regular departments and divisions take care of it." All these illustrate the pragmatism with which faculties and administrators not infrequently and uniquely clothe continuing education as they confront program priorities and resource allocations.

If the above constitutes the general academic context of the parent university, what strategies are suggested for strengthening continuing education support?

Surely, of first order of importance is to join effectively in the selection of a new president and chief executive officer of the university itself. Given the inward-facing tendencies and strengths of the collegial mode, the outlooks held by such officers about university functions are of exceptional importance. Just as the founding of major continuing education centers often reflected the commitment and leadership of college presidents (for example, Harper of Chicago, Van Hise of Wisconsin), present support of continuing education is not likely to endure and be enhanced by parent universities unless the chief executive supports extending the learning enterprise into the wider world. Indeed, it is most likely that swings in priority, intention, organization, and flair of higher adult education coincide, in no small way, with changes of university presidents. Accordingly, just as other campus groups will seek to influence such selections, each believing that a particular field is at stake, so should continuing educators and their support groups be always ready for what has become an all too rapid changing of university presidents.

Of no less importance is the selection of the *campus director* or dean for continuing education. Each academic institution has its special criteria for defining administrative capacities, including competence and related credentials, experience and accompanying achievements, and definable capabilities for performing expected tasks. Accordingly, perhaps more than any post besides president, selection of the continuing education director, who must mobilize campus-wide interest, requires participation beyond the central administration and continuing education staff. Adroitness with involving significant others on the selection committees, careful attention to interview schedules for candidates, collection of wide reactions and suggestions, and the manner of representing the candidates as campus-wide leaders, all are important in the recruitment and selection process.

Moreover, it is worth realizing that institutional support of continuing education will to a great degree depend upon how its director will interpret the field to central administration and fellow administrators. The director will need or will have to develop such skills, an achievement that is patently more important than seeking to enlarge support on a day-by-day basis when the director cannot lead it. Does he or she have the personal strength to gain and sustain access to central administration? Is he or she of commensurable presence in the company of other campus deans and directors? Does the director possess sufficient credentials and involvements that he or she is viewed as more than a mechanical administrator of courses, credits, and classrooms, viewed, rather, as a person of professional influence beyond the campus itself? Does the director possess that special capacity for language and its forceful use to interpret the campus and community worlds to each other? Such questions only suggest those skills without which, when the local director fails to possess or develop them, most other strategies to enhance the support of the parent university will very likely abort.

In mounting a sustained plan to enhance institutional support of continuing education, careful attention must always be paid those *groups external* to the univesity to which continuing educators have natural access. As the level of formal education attainment in American society increases, it is axiomatic that ever greater proportions of the citizenry will be desirous of both credit and noncredit opportunities for further learning. At the same time, if the overall growth of population continues to slow, it seems certain that American colleges and universities will find it necessary to address more and different categories of learners. Thus, in no way intended as strategies of pressure, support of continuing education in the university system is likely to become increasingly responsive to the widening and deepening interests of the public in further education. The university as a learning haven for the young is a model that has already collapsed;

yet the positive cultivation of public understanding of new conceptions seems to be only partially achieved by continuing educators.

Trustees, administrators, and faculty leaders of universities sometimes fail to see the connection between their pursuit of donors and patrons and the extent and quality of continuing education programs. It is the task of continuing educators to help them make such connections, and to foster the strategies and mechanisms for doing so. Long-range planning committees, for university-wide as well as continuing education development, need to invite citizens to participate. Continuing educators should seek to include eloquent representatives of evening or other adult programs, people who will bring to the attention of trustees and administrators the importance of continuing education to themselves and others. Indeed, local directors of continuing education should keep up-to-date rosters of successful "graduates" of continuing education programs and work to have them included in important university groups—board of trustees, visiting committees, fund-raising organizations, alumni councils, and the many advisory committees which have come to characterize most colleges and universities.

In addition, the continuing education agency may sponsor imaginative groups, events, and processes which enlist the talents of its own graduates and associates. These might include visiting committees for continuing education, thematic conferences and retreats of adult learners and graduates (to which traditional faculty and administrators are invited), volunteer assistance by citizen friends of continuing education to special university efforts, as in fund-raising, alumni weekends, and special observances (whether to celebrate an institutional birthday or to inaugurate a new president). Such initiatives are intended to define the students, graduates, and friends of continuing education as everyday members of the institutional family, not as members of the separated, uninterested, preoccupied off-campus world they frequently are believed to be.

The previous three strategies to enhance support of continuing education by the parent university will serve to influence the overall place and the importance of the field as part of the university's future. They are rather indirect strategies: they aim but obliquely at financial and organizational support. They seek instead to identify continuing education with the overall purposes and conduct of the university.

However, direct strategies are also important within such an interactive framework. To interpret diligently and creatively the promise of continuing education—to its own learners and to the university as a whole—is perhaps the major task of the local director and, to the extent possible, of all other continuing educators on the campus. This will properly include periodic reviews of the program with the president and staff of central administration, careful arrangement of similar encounters with other deans and directors, preparation of reports and digests which creatively depict what is happening locally and how it relates to the cutting edge of the continuing education movement, and distribution of media-centered information to alert and inform both the general public and the campus community.

Despite the seemingly recalcitrant views of traditional faculties and the frequent financial limitations (faculty overload arrangements, pay-as-you-go plans, policy uncertainty for noncredit programs, and insufficient risk capital), continuing educators must strive to sustain an adequate colleagueship with others on the campus.

This must begin with determination from the continuing educator to overcome status uncertainties, often requiring almost psychological conversion, and to insist firmly that the field is important in itself, and to the university. It is quite necessary to believe that its substance is sufficient to assure partnership with faculty from other disciplines and professions. The continuing educator must have something important to say in the academic arena, lest he or she is seen as a facilitator of a substance possessed by others.

The collegial spirit is strengthened when the continuing educator devises means for widespread participation of faculty and administrators in planning and conducting programs. For example, joint advisory committees can introduce traditional faculties to graduates, students, adjunct faculty, and friends of continuing education. New programs can be shared with other departments and divisions before they are initiated. Incentives can be devised to interest faculty in preparing for, and then taking part in new program efforts (attending workshops and conferences or providing seed dollars for developing a unique presentation), and offering opportunities for observation and research in field situations. In brief, the continuing educator will be striving day-by-day to enlarge the campus circle of those with whom he or she is working, of those who are on the way to comprehending the field (especially other directors and deans), of those who, given carefully arranged circumstances, will step forward to assist.

One aim of fostering this circle of campus interest is to secure the proper administrative and organizational position for continuing education. While its exact form may vary widely, it is difficult to see how the field can hold its own and perform its tasks without an appropriate location in the table of organization. Two questions must, of course, be answered: how best may this total university's mission be served and how best may continuing education be arranged to accomplish its special tasks.

Three principles come to mind: (1) continuing education needs its own organization, budget, and personnel to include, if possible, its own faculty core, whether housed together or dispersed; (2) joint appointments should be developed so that university-wide links may be forged; and (3) once such a dependable identity is assured, other departments should be encouraged to mount programs of continuing education (and the personnel to conduct them) within some reasonable plan of coordination.

If the university is to become enthusiastic in its support of continuing education, all parts of it must be involved. However, the traditional constraints have proven so enduring that not very much is likely to happen without an assigned source of forceful leadership and example. Indeed, under some such principles as above, the continuing education unit might well be the center for new efforts in continuing education and community educational service, with the understanding that much of its effort would be spread, sponsored, and augmented throughout the university. It is both a mood and a model that calls for reasonable and durable support from the center, a measure of risk capital, and a sense of personal and professional security on the part of continuing educators.

The foregoing statement suggests that enhancing support of the continuing education agency by the parent university depends first on establishing university leaders and missions which willingly and vigorously espouse the propriety of continuing education, university outreach, and community educational service. Rational planning is required for interactive and organizational ventures between continuing educators and significant others, both in and out of the university (Michael, 1973). It is a process that is especially sensitive to centers of leadership—in university administration, in the faculty-at-large, and in the evolving client groups upon which continuing education necessarily depends. The overall outcome is a political achievement in the best sense of the term.

References

Baldridge, J. V., Curtis, D. V., Ecker, G., and Riley, G. L. *Policy Making and Effective Leadership: A National Study of Academic Management.* San Francisco: Jossey-Bass, 1978.

Farmer, J. A., Jr., and Knox, A. B. *Alternative Patterns for Strengthening Community Service Programs in Institutions of Higher Education.* Urbana: Office for the Study of Continuing Professional Education, University of Illinois at Urbana-Champaign, 1977.

Michael, D. N. *On Learning to Plan—and Planning to Learn: The Social Psychology of Changing Toward Future-Responsive Societal Learning.* San Francisco: Jossey-Bass, 1973.

Reeves, M. "The European University from Medieval Times, with Special Reference to Oxford and Cambridge." In W. R. Niblett (Ed.), *Higher Education: Demand and Response.* London: Tavistock, 1969.

Paul A. Miller is President Emeritus and professor of science and humanities, Rochester Institute of Technology, New York State.

*Any plan to increase the resource allocations to
continuing education should optimize social,
psychological, and political forces that potentially
influence the campus decision-making process.*

Strengthening Collegiate Financial Support for Continuing Education

Dennis A. Dahl
Robert G. Simerly

The growth and vitality of a collegiate continuing education program frequently depends upon the willingness of the campus to provide adequate financial support. This support may take many forms. For example, it may involve increasing faculty pay for extension teaching, adding staff for new or expanded program activities, or increasing salary and expense budgets to support greater numbers of credit or noncredit programs. This chapter examines the traditional strategy used by continuing educators to strengthen campus financial support and then suggests a more appropriate strategy based upon the planned change models described in Chapter Two of the sourcebook.

The Traditional Approach

The traditional approach for gaining increased financial support for continuing education is to present a request which is supported by good evidence and sound reasons. This is typically true whether we are approaching our own institution or some external funding source, such as a private foundation or a government agency. Usually, the key to success is assumed to be a proposal that is so compelling in its logic and supporting evidence that it becomes impossible to deny.

The traditional strategy for strengthening campus financial support goes something like this. Someone within the continuing education agency decides that there is a need for more money for a particular aspect of the program. He or she sits down either alone or with other members of the continuing education staff and develops a proposal for the increased support. This proposal contains a thorough description of the problem, an analysis of how the requested resources will help overcome the problem, and the benefits that will result for both adult students and the campus if the request is granted.

Once the proposal satisfies the continuing education staff, it is submitted to the campus administration for consideration. This submission process may involve the continuing education dean or director personally delivering the proposal to the campus chancellor or vice-chancellor for academic affairs and discussing at length the merits of the proposal. Just as often, the proposal is simply transmitted to the appropriate campus official with a cover letter from the dean or director that indicates support. The point is that, in either case, the proposal in itself is thought to be so compelling that it, standing alone, will guarantee support. Once the proposal has been submitted, the continuing education office typically sits back and waits for a decision.

The problem with this approach is that often a strong argument alone is not enough. This is particularly true during periods of financial stringency when the campus receives hundreds of requests for increased financial support and, no matter how compelling the argument, simply cannot afford to grant them all. Given this situation, continuing educators who hope to increase financial support for continuing education need to look beyond creating a powerfully reasoned and documented argument for this increased support. They must broaden their focus and their strategy to include not only the logic and rationality of the argument itself but also the conditions under which the argument is developed, communicated, and received.

The traditional approach for gaining increased financial support has two fundamental weaknesses. First, the case for increased support is often developed in isolation from those at the campus level who will finally decide. Second, the approach assumes that organizations make financial decisions in a rational sequence of activities based upon reason and evidence. In this regard, continuing educators have discovered all too often that this is not the case.

The Social Systems Approach

The social systems approach to strengthening financial support begins with the assumption that organizational decision making is influenced not only by sound evidence and reason but also by social, psychological, and political forces that exist within the organization and also in the external environment. If continuing educators are to strengthen campus financial support for continuing education, they need to understand these forces and build them into their strategy. Chapter Two describes factors that are associated with successful planned organizational change. Several of these factors assume particular importance when developing a social systems approach for increasing financial support for continuing education. They are described below through the use of an example.

Assume that a continuing education administrator wants to increase faculty salaries for continuing education teaching and that this increase will require additional financial support from the campus. The decision to approve the funds for such an increase rests with the vice-chancellor for academic affairs. The first step in developing a social systems approach for gaining this increased support would likely be to convene a small group of persons from around the campus who share a commitment to this goal and who would be willing to assist in developing a strategy for its achievement. Ideally, this group should have a good understanding of the need for increased support, enjoy a high level of esteem among their faculty and administrative colleagues, possess the expertise to address the problem, and have the time to devote to the effort. In the case of our example, it would make sense to involve a representative from the vice-chancellor's office as well as a budget expert in this initial planning process. In addition, it would be helpful to have several senior faculty members involved in the planning group, particularly if they are held in high esteem by the vice-chancellor. Once the planning group is formed, they can begin to address the following questions.

What exactly do we want to accomplish in the way of increased faculty salaries for continuing education teaching? How much of an increase is needed? Is this figure realistic given current campus financial problems? If not, could the necessary increase be proposed in incremental stages over the next several years? Should the increase disproportionately benefit a particular faculty rank? For example, should assistant professors receive a disproportionately higher increase compared to full professors or vice versa? What would be the effects of such an increase? All of these questions relate to the process of defining precisely what needs to be accomplished. Those proposing the increased support need to have a thorough knowledge of what they are proposing and how it will affect various constituent groups throughout the campus.

Where will we find support for increasing faculty salaries for continuing education teaching? Are there supporters who can assist in providing leadership for achieving our goal? Are some of the supporters of such an increase well placed to influence the decision-making process? Conversely, who is likely to object to such an increase? What is the basis for their objection? Can these objections be dealt with effectively? Each time a shift is made in campus financial support, some people lose while others gain. It is important to understand this effect and anticipate ways of dealing with it. In this regard, it is useful to invite input from critics as well as advocates of increased financial support.

How do we stand in relation to what other institutions pay their faculty for continuing education teaching? Are there other institutions that have recently increased such stipends? If so, how did they go about it and what can they teach us? This linkage with others who have successfully addressed the same problem can be invaluable in providing insights and suggestions regarding the best course of action.

Can we link the need to increase faculty salaries for continuing education teaching with the central traditions, priorities, or needs of the campus? For example, is there a strong tradition of campus continuing education and public service? Is there a need to build public support for the campus or sharpen the public perception that the campus is making a considerable contribution to the state or region? If increased financial support can be linked to a strong institutional priority or need, it stands a much better chance of being approved.

Who stands to gain from increasing faculty salaries for continuing education teaching? Clearly, those faculty who teach adults will benefit but how about others? For example, certain departments and colleges may benefits needs to be explored before proposing additional financial support continuing education. The chancellor and president may also profit by being able to demonstrate to public policy makers that the campus is making a significant commitment to continuing education in the state. In this sense, there may be a political advantage for the entire institution if there is more continuing education. The point is that the full range of benefits need to be explored before proposing additional financial support for continuing education. It is upon the sum of these benefits that a strong case can be built.

Is the timing right for a proposal to increase faculty salaries for continuing education teaching? Are there forces at work on the campus or in the external environment that make this the best (or worst) time to make such a proposal? Often a proposal to increase financial support can be doomed to failure because of poor timing. This fact underscores the need to have someone on the planning team who understands the campus budgetary and decision-making process who can advise on matters related to timing.

How can we gain the support of key campus leaders and have them feel a sense of ownership for the proposal to increase financial support? One way is to involve them in the problem at an early stage. Discuss the situation with them. Let them suggest solutions and then build those suggestions into the final proposal. Ideally, they should see the problem as theirs as well as yours and they should feel a commitment to its resolution. This is most easily accomplished if they are involved early in the problem-solving process and their suggestions are included in the final proposal. After all, it is much more difficult to reject a proposal that oneself helped generate.

The advantage of the social systems approach to strengthening financial support is that it involves much more than simply developing and submitting a thorough and comprehensive proposal. In the social system approach, those campus officials who will ultimately make the decision are involved in the earliest stages of the problem-solving process; key campus opinion leaders help make the case; the proposal itself is linked to campus priorities, traditions, and needs; supporters of the proposed increase from across the campus are identified and share in developing and implementing the planned change process; input is solicited from opponents as a way of better understanding their perspectives and determining the strength of their position; coalitions of supporters are formed; timing of the request is judged in terms of institutional factors that may influence decision makers' attitudes toward the proposal. In short, the social systems approach encourages the development of a strategy for increasing support that includes attention to the whole range of institutional and environmental forces that can influence the decision-making process.

The disadvantage of the social systems approach is that it is often far more time consuming than the traditional approach. It also requires a level of organizational understanding that many continuing educators do not possess. However, we believe that if the goal is to strengthen campus financial support for continuing education, the social systems approach offers far greater chance for success than the traditional approach used on most campuses.

This chapter has attempted to apply the planned change perspective developed in Chapter Two to suggest a social systems approach to increase the share of the college budget allocated to continuing education. In periods of financial stringency, campus administrators simply are not able to provide support for all of the requests that they receive, no matter how compelling the logic or thorough the evidence. In this context, a well-developed proposal is often not enough. The social systems approach takes a total systems view of the organization and considers those social, psychological, and political forces which added to logic and reason influence the decision-making process.

*Dennis A. Dahl is director of the Office of
Continuing Education and Public Service and
associate vice-chancellor for academic affairs at the
University of Illinois at Urbana-Champaign.*

Robert G. Simerly is head of the Conferences and Institutes Division, Office of Continuing Education and Public Service at the University of Illinois at Urbana-Champaign.

Continuing Education will never be a central university mission until integrated into the primary faculty reward system.

Strengthening Collegiate Faculty Rewards for Continuing Education

Donald E. Hanna

Incentives and rewards for faculty members who participate in continuing education activities are critical to ensure the success of any university outreach mission. Yet, in most universities a faculty member's involvement in these activities is scarcely considered when decisions are made regarding his or her promotion, tenure, or salary status (Centra, 1977; Hohenstein, 1980; Seldin, 1975). Recognizing this, many faculty members understandably shy away from participating in continuing education, concentrating instead on activities that "count" and are more consistent with discipline-related values (McCarthy, 1980).

Faced with a faculty reluctant to participate in continuing education as a regular assignment, many universities have either developed alternative incentives and rewards (including separate, but less powerful, extrinsic rewards such as overload pay) or separate faculties who devote all of their time to outreach and are rewarded independently of the traditional faculty. However, these methods are generally recognized as subordinate to the institution's primary reward system and do little to change faculty perceptions of the value of continuing education. They may in fact reinforce the marginality of such efforts by providing an alternative means of reward. Additional limitations of separate reward mechanisms are noted by Knox (1975), Patton (1975), Hanna (1978), and Votruba (1978). At best, they can be described as necessary but not sufficient incentives in the research-oriented university.

The theme that continuing education is given minimal attention within the regular reward system is common throughout the literature (Gordon, 1974; Hanna, 1978; Knox, 1975; Patton, 1975). In a survey of continuing education administrators, McCarthy (1980) found that almost half of her sample indicated that community service/continuing education was not part of faculty evaluation criteria at their institutions. University of Illinois faculty members with experience on promotion and tenure committees support this view, indicating that evaluation of the quality of outreach efforts in promotion and tenure papers is sketchy, if present at all. As a result, outreach performance rarely contributes to a positive promotion and tenure decision.

The dimensions of this problem are clearly important to university administrators charged with attracting and applying the full resources of the faculty to educational needs and problems of individuals and communities. Indeed, Votruba (1978) argues that unless outreach activities are more fully integrated into the primary faculty reward system and accepted as criteria for salary, promotion, and tenure decisions, continuing education and public service stand little chance of achieving more than peripheral status in the university.

This chapter describes a project under way at the University of Illinois at Urbana-Champaign which has three interrelated goals: (1) the development of criteria for evaluating the quality of faculty efforts in continuing education and public service; (2) the utilization of these criteria by faculty members engaged in outreach activities; and (3) the acceptance of these criteria by faculty and academic administrators who are involved in the campus salary, promotion, and tenure evaluation process.

In the 1970s, the University of Illinois at Urbana-Champaign began to devote increasing attention to encouraging faculty participation in continuing education and public service. Several factors contributed to this increased attention, including changing population demographics, the need to more visibly demonstrate public service to the citizens of Illinois, an increase in the number of academic departments involved in continuing education, and direct support from campus administrators. The combination of these factors resulted in the strengthening of institutional policy to give greater support and legitimacy to faculty outreach activities. For example, in 1973 the campus senate endorsed the following resolutions: "Campus and college-level procedures should be modified so that there are greater incentives and rewards for high-quality faculty participation as resource persons in university-sponsored continuing education and public service activities."

In 1975, the vice-chancellor for academic affairs established a faculty committee to advise the campus on how rewards for both teaching and service could be strengthened. His charge to the committee made clear that high-quality continuing education activities alone could never assure a successful promotion or tenure decision:

> I am not asking the committee to develop procedures or a rationale for a multi-track system in which one might be promoted on the basis of teaching or research or service. In my view (and the Campus Committee on Promotion and Tenure appears to agree) research, scholarship, and creative artistry of high quality must be demonstrated if one is to successfully be recommended for promotion and indefinite tenure. However, in many instances outstanding performance in teaching and/or service, if the case is well documented, can result in a favorable outcome when the record of scholarship is not quite sufficient.

The final report of the Committee on Teaching and Service demonstrated concern for documentation of quality of faculty outreach activities by providing a framework for identifying criteria and sources of evidence to use in evaluation of these activities.

In the fall of 1978, the vice-chancellor for academic affairs again addressed the issue of evaluation of faculty outreach efforts: "The reward system for continuing education in public service is important, and we do have in the process at Urbana-Champaign a section in the promotion and tenure process dealing with that area. As I read those sections each year, I have the feeling that many people seem to be engaged in such activity but that none of it is evaluated. The activity of the Urbana-Champaign faculty, by and large, is not rewarded in this area because nobody bothers to tell the administration or to find out whether they do a good job or not; this is a serious problem. We must, if this is to be a part of the promotion and tenure process, find a way of assessing the quality of that work just as we do for on-campus instruction, scholarly work, creative artistry, and the rest of what goes into promotion and tenure." Clearly, the vice-chancellor's remarks indicated that more systematic evaluation of faculty outreach activities would be required to significantly contribute to a successful promotion and tenure decision.

Faculty Reward Project

In the fall of 1978, a four-person project team combining administrators and instructors was formed within the Office of Continuing Education and Public Service to more effectively relate faculty outreach activities to the campus promotion and tenure system. Four specific objectives were defined:

1. Development of an evaluative approach which could be used to assess the quality of faculty outreach efforts.

2. Development of a sense of commitment to, and ownership for, this evaluative approach at the departmental, college, and campus levels.
3. Application of this approach to specific faculty outreach activities.
4. Evaluation of this approach and dissemination of the findings throughout the university.

The strategy selected by the project team to accomplish these objectives was based upon organizational change theory, drawing heavily from Havelock (1973), Lindquist (1978), and Votruba (1978). Characteristics of successful planned change (described in Chapter Two of this sourcebook) provided guidance in selecting and establishing priorities for project team activities. During the early stages of the project, organization and leadership were particularly important considerations for the project team as was the degree of commitment and willingness of each member to devote substantial time to pursuing the project's goals and objectives. As plans for the project developed, other characteristics of successful planned change became important and are sumarized below.

Relating Change to Faculty Values. Universities are conservative in their orientation to and capacity for organizational change. This serves to heighten the importance of carefully relating intended changes to the dominant values and traditions of the faculty. This is particularly true when dealing with something as fundamental to the institution as its faculty reward system. Recognizing the difficulty of major change in this setting, the project team defined the project so that its conceptual base and goals were closely related to the accepted values of the faculty, suggesting that continuing education and public service are more appropriately considered as parts of the traditional faculty functions of teaching and scholarship than as conceptually distinct forms of professional activity. The project team defined continuing education activities as essentially off-campus forms of teaching, and public service as an applied form of scholarship, thereby relating each more closely to widely understood and accepted faculty values. This proximity to the institution's primary mission and values enhanced the probability of faculty acceptance of the project's goals.

Ownership of the Project's Goals. Expanding ownership of the project's goals was essential and required the active involvement of decision makers across the campus, including the vice-chancellor for academic affairs, deans and department heads, and promotion and tenure committee members at all levels. Early activities designed to achieve this invovlement included extensive discussions with the following individuals and groups: (1) vice-chancellor for academic affairs, (2) past and present members of campus promotion and tenure committees, (3) deans and associate deans of selected colleges and heads of academic departments with substantial outreach involvement, (4) the faculty senate committee on continuing education and public service, (5) the campus council on continuing education and public service, and (6) individual faculty members who had recently prepared promotion and tenure papers. In addition, a committee from the campus council on continuing education and public service was formed to provide assistance and guidance for the project. The project team used these discussions to offer information concerning the problem and to receive feedback on various steps that might be taken. Meetings also served to educate the project team concerning prevailing campus attitudes toward outreach activities and offered the opportunity to solicit involvement and support from a wide spectrum of faculty and administrators. Suggestions and comments received during this phase were invaluable in selecting an approach appropriate to the campus. The objective was and continues to be to encourage key people in the promotion and tenure process to develop a sense of commitment to the project and its outcomes. Without this commitment, it is unlikely that the project can be an effective catalyst for change in the promotion and tenure process.

Creating an Open Environment. The early involvement of a large number of faculty members and academic administrators heightened awareness of the problem of strengthening institutional rewards for faculty participation in outreach activities and started internal discussion by promotion and tenure committees at all levels and by department executive committees. In several instances the project team was invited to department faculty meetings to explain the project and explore the possibility of working collaboratively with its junior faculty.

This sharing of information also provided an opportunity to learn more about faculty perceptions of why participation in continuing education is not more adequately rewarded and, in some cases, to be exposed to feelings about why outreach should *not* be rewarded through the promotion and tenure system. This information was of vital importance as the project team continually assessed the institutional climate in which the project is being conducted.

Benefits of the Project. If this approach is to be successful, those involved in the promotion and tenure process must perceive desired changes in the reward system as beneficial to them. Long-range potential for key participants, identified during the interview phase of the project, include the following. Faculty will more clearly understand continuing education and public service (resulting in a more systematic approach to selection of and participation in specific activities) and criteria for evaluating continuing education and public service activities will be clarified (resulting in stronger evidence of the quality of such activities). Promotion and tenure committees and the vice-chancellor for academic affairs benefit by more effective evaluation of quality of outreach activities, resulting in less ambiguity about their significance as factors in promotion and tenure decisions. They will also achieve clearer understanding of how outreach activities can contribute to successful promotion and tenure decisions, leading to an improvement in quality of promotion and tenure papers. Academic administrators will be better able to establish criteria for encouraging some forms of outreach activities and discouraging others, thereby strengthening the quality, direction, and focus of department and college efforts. Facilitation of clearer communication between department heads and faculty members regarding the promotion and tenure process in general is another likely benefit. Continuing education administrators, themselves, will discover greater willingness of faculty members to participate in and support outreach activities, resulting in more visible and effective service to the state, and improvement of the quality of faculty activities in continuing education and public service.

While these benefits are clearly long range rather than immediate, their significance is indicated by the support each group has provided for the project to date. And to the extent that these groups benefit from greater consideration of high-quality outreach efforts, the university and the clientele it serves through outreach activities also gain.

Linkages with Other Resources. Developing linkages with other information resources has been an integral part of the project team's activities. For example, more than 300 campus promotion and tenure papers submitted in previous years, both successful and unsuccessful, were reviewed during the first year of the project. The purpose of this review was to identify important characteristics of successful and unsuccessful papers. Apparent strengths and weaknesses of papers were checked for validity with promotion and tenure committee members, and their identification represents one of the major findings of the project to date.

A communication network with other institutions and individuals who were looking at the problem also provided useful information. The project team gathered examples of official policy statements from other universities, organized a meeting of the Committee on Institutional Cooperation (Big Ten Universities and the University of Chicago) deans of continuing education to discuss the problem and the proposed approach, and presented findings of the project at regional and national conferences. These activities facilitated contact with other professionals concerned with or actively working on increased faculty participation in continuing education.

Project Outcomes

A detailed study of which outreach activities and which sources of judgment are given greatest consideration in promotion and tenure decisions is currently under way with formal sponsorship of the vice-chancellor for academic affairs. This information along with that collected from earlier interviews will be distributed in the form of a faculty guide to all department heads to share with newly appointed faculty members. The guide will be brief (10–15 pages) and will emphasize the importance of

(1) early agreement between the faculty member and department chair regarding the nature of participation in continuing education and public service and methods of assessing quality; (2) evaluation of the quality of faculty participation in outreach activities in addition to the quantity; (3) selection of outreach activities that can be evaluated according to institutionally valued criteria; and (4) encouraging new faculty members to consider preparation for promotion and tenure decisions early and to relate their choice of outreach activities to the promotion and tenure process. In this regard, four steps are recommended: (1) faculty members should consult early with the chair concerning departmental expectations regarding outreach activities and the criteria upon which activities will be evaluated; (2) faculty members should schedule outreach involvement that links outreach efforts to professional and personal goals and the promotion and tenure process; (3) specific outreach activities should be identified along with criteria for evaluation; and (4) papers should be prepared stressing the demonstrated quality of outreach activities. Each of these steps should be taken in close consultation with the department chair and others important in the promotion and tenure process.

In addition to the development of the faculty guide, the project team plans to work with individual faculty members involved extensively in outreach activities, focusing on alternative ways of evaluating outreach activities and methods of organizing and presenting evaluative data in promotion and tenure papers.

The Faculty Rewards Project is based on the assumption that continuing education will never truly be a central mission of universities until fully integrated into the primary faculty reward structure. This integrative process presents a complex and formidable challenge for which success is far from assured. Nevertheless, it is a problem that continuing educators must address if they are to make continuing education and public service a more significant mission of the university.

This project has as its major goal effecting change in the promotion and tenure system to more adequately recognize and reward quality faculty participation in continuing education and public service. The project is progressing because its goals appear to be important to the campus administration, including academic deans, department heads, and promotion and tenure committees. The eventual success of this project will depend on the extent to which (1) the findings from the first stages of the project can be applied in helping faculty members to improve decisions about selection and evaluation of outreach activities and (2) presentation of these activities in promotion and tenure papers contributes to a positive promotion and tenure decision. Although it is too early to gauge the long-term outcomes of the project, the approach used by the project team may serve as a guide for continuing educators in university settings who face this fundamental problem.

References

Centra, J. A. *How Universities Evaluate Faculty Performance: A Survey of Department Heads.* Princeton, N.J.: Educational Testing Service, 1977.

Gordon, M. "The Organization of Continuing Education in Universities and Colleges." *NUEA Spectator,* 1974, *37,* 20-27.

Hanna, D. E. "Faculty Participation in Continuing Education: A Case Study." Unpublished doctoral dissertation, Michigan State University, 1978.

Havelock, R. G. *The Change Agent's Guide to Innovation in Education.* Englewood Cliffs, N.J.: Educational Technology Publications, 1973.

Hohenstein, W. V. "Service: The Neglected Person of the Academic Trinity." *National Forum,* 1980, *40,* 18-19.

Knox, A. "New Realities: The Administration of Continuing Higher Education." *NUEA Spectator,* 1975, *39,* 6-9.

Lindquist, J. *Strategies for Change.* Washington, D.C.: Council for the Advancement of Small Colleges, 1978.

McCarthy, M. B. "Continuing Education Service as a Component of Faculty Evaluation." *Lifelong Learning: The Adult Years,* 1980, *3,* (9), 8-11.

Patton, C. V. "Extended Education in an Elite Institution: Are There Sufficient Incentives to Encourage Faculty Participation?" *Journal of Higher Education,* 1975, *46,* 427-444.

Seldin, P. *How Colleges Evaluate Professors.* Croton-on-Hudson, N.Y.: Blythe-Pennington, 1975.

Votruba, J. C. "Faculty Rewards for University Outreach: An Integrative Approach." *Journal of Higher Education,* 1978, *49,* 639-648.

Donald E. Hanna is head of the Extramural Courses Division in the Office of Continuing Education and Public Service and assistant professor of continuing education at the University of Illinois at Urbana-Champaign.

Continuing education administrators and student services personnel should provide stronger leadership and planned change strategies to strengthen support services for adult students.

Strengthening Collegiate Adult Student Services

Judith A. Riggs

Student services in continuing education are often the last area to receive programming attention or financial allocations. Those who provide student services should take a more active role in broadening organizational support for this function if continuing education programs are going to be truly responsive to the adult student.

Continuing education programs typically provide few, if any, support services for adult students. The task of bringing about change often appears overwhelming because of the number of concerns that need to be addressed. These include: (1) providing support services in the evening hours—admissions, financial aid, registration, academic advisement, career counseling, and testing and placement; (2) allowing campus resources to be available to other than registered degree-seeking students; (3) responding to students' personal concerns; and (4) providing evening hours and appointments with faculty members and administrators.

Planning Change Strategy

The first step in strengthening organizational support for adult-oriented student services is to identify the nature, scope, and relative importance of the various potential needs that can be addressed. What needs are most important for adults who now attend or might attend your institution? Use your staff, colleagues, and present students to help identify and prioritize these needs. As an example, at the University of Southern California, the concept of evening college services developed after faculty, staff, and students in the College of Continuing Education expressed the need for student services similar to those that day students were receiving.

Read the adult education literature regarding perceptions of experts and other practitioners about student service needs of adult students. (Good sources are Baille, Eignor, and Averill, 1976; Farmer, 1971; Havighurst and Orr, 1956; Knox, 1977; Porter, 1970; Riggs, 1980.)

Talk with practitioners and colleagues in other educational settings about their ideas; talk with adults themselves; and identify key people in your community or state who work with potential participants to obtain their thoughts.

In organizations where there are several offices that provide continuing education, first test your ideas for strengthening support within your own offices before going to outside faculty and staff. Enlist the support of your own staff and include those who are most interested in augmenting support services to help design and implement the change strategy. You may find that organizational commitment has to be developed within your own staff before approaching others in the parent organization. For example, if you want to begin providing academic counseling to adult students who are taking credit courses in an off-campus location, you first should consult with the appropriate departments in continuing education and the academic units in which the off-campus students are enrolled. If the continuing education departments or the academic units do not feel their students need academic counseling or if they do not wish to contribute to the funding or programming of such support services, the change that you want should not be proposed to the parent organization until it is accepted internally by both groups. Otherwise, you may find yourself in the middle of a situation in which you are asking for parent organizational support but where, in fact, your own continuing education colleagues are saying the support is not necessary.

Colleagues within your continuing education agency who agree with your suggestions for change can be invaluable in generating alternatives and planning strategies, in helping you understand and gain support from decision makers in the parent organization, and in implementing the final change solution.

Especially if you work in a small institution, or are the only continuing education administrator, you should work within the organization to find faculty members and student service personnel who are interested in working on your team. An example is provided by a women's program which was successfully implemented in a community college in Ilinois. A major part of the success in the acceptance and adoption of the program was the fact that the program coordinator (change agent) first discussed the idea with several counseling colleagues and the dean of students, gained support from several key women faculty members, and formed a strategy team to help plan the program and the ways to approach the administrators who would effect the change. Advocates within the senior faculty can be particularly valuable, especially if they represent academic programs that enroll large numbers of adult students.

Whether in a small or large organization, the needs that are identified should be ranked and perhaps several priority lists from different perspectives should be compiled. It is important to assess the climate in the parent organization and to avoid proposing more than you believe has a chance of being considered. Do not overwhelm the parent organization with every conceivable adult student support need, but begin the change effort with a few of the more important needs. Assuming initial success, other needs can be introduced later.

In order to bring about change more effectively, new and successful practices in student services such as those discussed by DiSilvestro (1979) should be considered and shared with the strategy team. You should also be aware of, and discuss with your team, external resources (people, organizations, and funding agencies) that should be considered or consulted before final strategy planning occurs.

It is important for the team leader and members of the planned change team to know and establish credibility with as many faculty members, administrators, and opinion leaders as possible. The change process should be discussed with the team and other colleagues because many of them will not be aware of the process and the relevance of each of the steps in the change process.

Improving Chances for Success

As the leader for planning organizational change for student services, it becomes important for you to recognize that you need to play various roles in the change process. Havelock (1973) defines these roles as catalyst, solution giver, process helper, and resource linker. (See also Chapter Two of this sourcebook.)

In feeling the pressure from the adult student to make some changes, you become the catalyst to prod and pressure the system to adapt. You act as a catalyst when you cause colleagues to become concerned about your student personnel problems and when you make the decision to form a strategy team.

In your role as solution giver, tread lightly. Where you are working with a team to develop and implement a strategy for strengthening adult student services, allow your team to work through the problem-solving process without dominating or always offering the solution. If the team is allowed to work with your guidance, with you in the role of process helper, often the solution that you would have given will be derived from the team's efforts. After you have helped to build a working relationship among team members, your role as a process helper in the diagnosis of the problem will be to assist the team in surveying the symptoms of the problem, interpreting the evidence and making inferences about underlying causes, and identifying areas of strength and greatest potential for change (Havelock and others, 1969). You should also guide the team in acquiring relevant resources and choosing the solution after they have considered implications from research, generated a range of solution ideas, and tested the solution for feasibility. As the team evolves a solution, they become advocates to help adopt, install, and evaluate the solution much more readily than if you had given the solution.

As resource linker, you should provide information related to matters such as external funding sources, new and innovative practices in the field, organizations and institutions that have tried similar solutions, and experts who have knowledge and skills in diagnosing problems.

Create a climate of openness, honesty, and genuineness in your team efforts (Lindquist, 1978). Be organized. Make sure that your team understands its role and what is to be accomplished.

In the end, it is your responsibility as team leader to assure that the alternatives generated and the final solutions are ideas that are compatible with the parent organization—its values, traditions, priorities, and needs. It is your responsibility to know the decision makers and the outcomes that they value.

Implementing Change Strategy

Once you and your strategy team have identified goals and designed an organizational strategy for achieving them, test your strategies on opinion leaders within your institution. Get their suggestions before you meet with the decision makers.

Your strategy should include a plan for change that has both short-term and long-range goals (Lindquist, 1978). Your plan should be as comprehensive as possible and include sections on cost of implementation, logistics and facility usage, and faculty and administration involvement and commitment. It should include parts and subparts that can be implemented a little at a time. If there is resistance you may even want to suggest a pilot program so that the organization does not have to make a long-term commitment.

At one major university, the implementation of comprehensive student services for adults who were not registered for credit was a change that administrators were unwilling to accept. However, the project concept was eventually accepted after it was suggested that a scaled-down pilot project be tried. Instead of hiring a number of counselors and offering brokering service across the state, a telephone project was begun in which information about career planning, financial aids, and admission was provided to nonmatriculated students. After a period of time and careful record keeping, the administration became more aware of the need for this service and agreed to the implementation of a modified plan.

With limited funding in most educational institutions and especially within continuing education agencies, a prime concern for most decision makers when presented with a new programming idea will be how to pay for it. Be sure that you have investigated external funding sources and, if possible, present funding alternatives and sources of seed money. Cost savings can often be achieved through the free or low cost usage of existing campus or community facilities, joint funding of personnel, and the use of graduate students and paraprofessionals. When the modified brokering plan mentioned in the previous paragraph was implemented, instead of hiring full-time counselors with masters degrees, CETA money was used and paraprofessional counselors were trained for the career counseling function of the project. Graduate students were used in the central office of the project to gather career information, conduct research, evaluate the services being offered, and assist in the training of the paraprofessional counselors.

Your strategy and plan should also include a listing of benefits to the continuing education agency and the parent organization. Too often when objectives and benefits of a support service project are listed, they are stated only in terms of the client and are not stated in terms of the organization itself. For example, improved student support services for returning students may result in the institution's being more attractive to prospective adult students and increasing retention of current students. Your strategy should include becoming familiar with the problems and goals of the organizational decision makers upon whom the change effort depends. If the proposed change reflects their priorities, it stands a far better chance of being accepted. One of your goals is to help the decision makers understand how they and the organization can benefit if your plan is accepted.

The way in which decision makers are approached regarding the planned change may affect its acceptance and implementation. Learn about the preferences and styles of the decision makers. Some people like to be approached with enthusiasm and others prefer a more staid, matter-of-fact presentation; some like to be consulted on a one-to-one basis, passing the information on to important others, but others prefer a group meeting where all of the people who will make the decision will hear the information at the same time; and some people like to make important decisions in the morning while others prefer the afternoon hours. All of this requires thorough knowledge of the parent organization and the decision makers within it.

Your chances for success in bringing about positive planned change in adult student service areas will depend on your willingness and ability to take the initiative and to play many roles in assisting your team to plan a well-designed, well-managed strategy for change. The chances of success are probably greatest in those situations where the decision makers are convinced that what is good for the adult student is also in the best interests of the parent organization.

References

Baille, D., Eignor, D., and Averill, D. *Non-Traditional Student Needs Assessment Project: A Survey of Non-Traditional Student Needs at University of Massachusetts; Amherst Campus.* Amherst: University of Massachusetts, 1976.

DiSilvestro, F. *Successful Student Services Practices in National University Extension Association Institutions.* Washington, D.C.: National University Extension Association, 1979.

Farmer, M. *Counseling Services for Adults in Higher Education.* Metuchen, N.J.: Scarecrow Press, 1971.

Havelock, R. *The Change Agent's Guide to Innovations in Education.* Englewood Cliffs, N.J.: Educational Technology Publications, 1973.

Havelock, R., and others. *Planning for Innovation Through the Utilization of Knowledge.* Ann Arbor, Mich.: Institute for Social Research, 1969.

Havighurst, R., and Orr, B. *Adult Education and Adult Needs.* Chicago: Center for the Study of Liberal Education for Adults, 1956.

Knox, A. B. *Adult Development and Learning: A Handbook on Individual Growth and Competence in the Adult Years for Education and the Helping Professions.* San Francisco: Jossey-Bass, 1977.

Lindquist, J. *Developing the College Curriculum.* Washington, D.C.: Council for the Advancement of Small Colleges, 1978.

Porter, L. "Adults Have Special Counseling Needs." *Adult Leadership,* 1970, *18,* 275–276.

Riggs, J. *Advising or Counseling Adults.* Champaign, Ill.: Office of Continuing Education and Public Service, 1980.

Sheehy, G. *Passages: Predictable Crises of Adult Life.* New York: Bantam Books, 1974.

Judith A. Riggs is head of marketing, Office of Continuing Education and Public Service, at the University of Illinois at Champaign-Urbana. She spent six years as a counselor in a community college, two years as a coordinator of a program for women, and three years as head of an adult career counseling project at the University of Illinois at Urbana-Champaign.

Community colleges share with more traditional collegiate institutions the need for stimulating continuing education.

Strengthening Continuing Education in Community Colleges

James F. Gollattscheck

The task of promoting continuing education is quite different in community colleges than in most other types of higher education institutions. In some ways, it is an easier task. Most community colleges by their very nature are close to their communities and generally well aware of community educational needs. Most community colleges are open door institutions and therefore serve a wide variety of people in the community. The average age of students enrolled in credit courses in many community colleges is now nearly thirty and part-time students equal or outnumber full-time students. A significant number attend only at night. Community colleges typically offer a wide array of noncredit courses to meet community educational needs and have a variety of programs for the community under the label of community services. In addition, traditional credit courses are often taught in such off-campus locations as secondary schools, churches, libraries, hospitals, and even prisons. There is not, therefore, a need to orient the institution to nontraditional students in order to improve continuing education. Indeed, the nontraditional student is an integral part of most community colleges.

It would appear at first glance that continuing education may not need strengthening in most community colleges. In fact, this is not the case. Today, one finds as much concern over the priority given to continuing education in community colleges as in other more traditional collegiate institutions.

What appears to be happening in community colleges is not just an effort to strengthen an already viable continuing education component but an attempt to unify and redirect the focus of the institution toward meeting the full spectrum of learning needs in the community. Colleges once content with a mission statement that gave equal attention to continuing education as one of its three primary but somewhat separate functions are now moving toward mission statements that reflect a concern for the lifelong learning needs of all the community, viewing university-transfer and occupational degree programs as simply different facets of the same institutional endeavor as continuing education. Edmund Gleazer, president of the American Association of Community and Junior Colleges, sums up factors impacting community college purposes in the 1980s with the following proposed mission statement: "To encourage and facilitate lifelong learning with community as process and product" (Gleazer, 1980, p. 16).

The extent of current community college involvement in the broad field of education beyond the traditional college credit course is reflected in a monograph (Brawer, 1980) in which the author surveys the educational activities of community colleges with reference to confusion in terms and overlap in definitions. Community colleges, she observes, are involved in programs they call adult education, lifelong learning, continuing education, community education, community-based education, and community services. To this can be added two newer terms, education for community renewal and education for community development. One can surmise from Brawer's material that the current community college scene resembles not so much an ivory tower as a Tower of Babel. It can also be observed, however, that such a situation does indicate a widespread commitment to and involvement in nontraditional, community-oriented educational programs.

The solution envisioned by Brawer also reflects current efforts to unify the missions of community colleges. She points out that past attempts to classify courses and activities into the above categories by course purpose has not been successful and recommends that student intent be the device used for classification. Thus the same biology course, for example, might be a university parallel course for a premed student, an occupational educational course for a horticultural technology student, and a continuing education course for someone in the community wishing to understand more about the problems of the environment. Further, all of these students might be sitting in the same class at the same time.

Community-Based Institutions

When continuing education is considered an integral part of the operation of the entire college then whatever strengthens the college strengthens continuing education and vice versa. The remainder of this chapter will deal primarily with ways in which institutions already involved with their communities and already providing a variety of services to their communities, including continuing education, can and are developing a more unified, less fragmented approach to meeting all of the educational needs of the community. These colleges are moving forward as whole institutions in their efforts to provide whatever services are needed by their constituents rather than through the building up of one component at the real or perceived expense of others. This, it would seem, is the real and immediate task for community colleges and while strengthening continuing education in community colleges might not be difficult, the redirection of institutions is not easy.

The term *community-based* will be used to describe those community colleges that are committed to the improvement of their total communities and the individuals in them through making opportunities for learning available to all. Further, the community-based college works with the community to accomplish this purpose. Gollattscheck and others (1976, p. 7) make the case that the community-based college "delivers the kinds of education community members want and need, not what pedagogues think is good for them. It does so at locations where the learners are, not where conventional college organizations indicate they should be. It is guided by open community participation in defining comprehensive learning needs, suggesting solutions, and facilitating delivery, not by the decisions of professional educators and governing boards alone." Ultimately the term community-based implies, more than anything else, a relationship between the educational institution and the community—a relationship in which the institution determines its direction and develops its programs through interaction with the community. In such an institution, continuing education would be just one of many types of programs aimed at meeting the educational needs of its constituencies.

How an institution gets there can be examined in three broad areas of activity—planning, conducting, and evaluating programs. The key to strengthening the college as a community-based institution lies in the above paragraph. All those involved with the college—faculty and administration, students, trustees, nonfaculty employees, and representatives of the community at large—should be involved in planning, conducting, and evaluating the programs of the community-based college. In no other way can the breadth and depth of the community college commitment be kept in the forefront throughout these activities.

Max Tadlock, the president of Monterey Peninsula College (California), states that

> No college can call itself community based until it is ready to step through its own open doors and out into the community for

mutual guidance, support, and participation. For the college wishing to explore the dimensions and implications in changing from its normal institutional focus to a community focus, the best processes themselves are community based. These processes enable the community resources to determine what is needed and how best to meet the needs [Tadlock, 1978, p. 7].

Tadlock's plan is one that a number of community colleges have used with excellent results. It reflects the approach to planned organizational change suggested by Lindquist and discussed in Chapter Two of this sourcebook. It involves an intensive planning conference attended by community and college personnel, all of whom have received in advance enough information about the college, its current mission, organization, and resources to enable them to participate actively and effectively in planning. According to Tadlock (pp. 10-11), the conference should accomplish the following goals:

1. To reexamine and restate, if necessary, the mission of the institution.
2. To validate the profile of the institution and the community.
3. To determine what specific resources of the community and the college can and should be mobilized to meet community and individual needs.
4. To determine ways to optimize the educational services potential of the community through the agency of the college and other institutions.
5. To set priorities for any changes indicated.
6. To construct an action plan for initiating major operational and programmatic changes.
7. To secure commitments from both community and college participants to support and participate in the changes called for.

As in the old saying about the proof in the pudding, it is, of course, the nature and the qualities of the program offered that ultimately determine whether or not a college is community based and, therefore, has a strong continuing education component. If the planning has been sound and has been a joint endeavor between college personnel and representatives of the community, there should be a solid base of information about both the college and the community, including the needs and resources of each, upon which the college can build its programs, courses, and activities. The college must move cautiously, particularly if it has not had much experience in nontraditional offerings, because failures are costly both in terms of money and in terms of credibility. But, the college must move. It must begin to demonstrate to the community and to the college the fruits of its planning. Becoming community based is a little like the chicken and egg conundrum. A college may not be truly community based until the community perceives the college as having those characteristics; but, it cannot be perceived as being community based until it begins to show that it is. The reverse is also true. The more a college demonstrates its ability and willingness to meet a range of community educational needs, the more it will find itself called upon by the community to perform educational services.

The planning conference should have provided goals and objectives agreed upon by both college and community participants and an up-to-date community needs assessment, all of which can serve as guides to the college as it develops its programs. The best approach is to begin with activities that are clearly based on identified needs, consistent with group adopted goals and objectives, and within the ability of the college to offer successfully. In Florida, the success of programs offered through state-provided Community Instructional Service funds is relatively assured because built into the process through which courses and activities qualify for such funds is a survey to determine "high-priority community problems."

There is a somewhat natural tendency for a complex organization to splinter because both providers and consumers become very involved in their own specific areas of activity. As a result, community-based programs may sometimes be regarded as separate from the *real college* program, the real college program referring to the more traditional, degree-oriented, credit courses. In order that the college may move forward as a totally community-based institution, attention must be given to continued reinforcement of the concept that the college program is unified. If providing for the lifelong learning needs of the community is the unifying mission of the institution, both college and community need to be reminded from time to time that a premed transfer program, an occupational nursing program, a continuing education activity for health professionals, and a noncredit seminar in nutrition for senior citizens are merely different ways of providing for the lifelong learning needs of those in the community. The connecting links are sometimes forgotten and need to be emphasized.

In addition to legal requirements for accountability, community-based programs need to be evaluated for three compelling reasons. One, the strengths and weaknesses of any specific activity must be known if improvements are to be made. Two, the strengths and weaknesses of the community-based operation of the college as a whole must be identified if that operation is to be sustained. Three, the community's perception of the institution as an educational service available to it cannot be strengthened unless the institution can document its successes.

While much more needs to be said about the unique problems of evaluating nontraditional community-based programs than can be included in this chapter, one particular point needs to be made. When a commitment has been made to serve the educational needs of a broad spectrum of the community and to help solve a broad range of community problems, evaluation needs to go beyond assessing how well activities are carried out. The college must look also at what it has not done. The institution needs to ask not just how well it serves the elderly, for example, but what other constituencies did it not serve. Looking at what has not been done has not usually been a part of educational evaluation. Higher education has for so long been responsible for educating those who not only sought its services but who could qualify for them that measuring relative success by considering those for whom it did not provide learning experiences is not easy. There are few, if any, models. Yet, if a community-based institution is to hope to convince its supporters to provide resources to expand its programs, unmet needs must be documented. The community-based institution needs to ask:

- Who is attending its activities and why?
- What can it find out about those who are not attending?
- What identifiable constituencies in the community is it not serving and why?
- Is it fulfilling all elements of its mission, goals, and objectives?

A most important area of assessment for a community-based institution is the image of the college in the community. As was pointed out earlier, the institution that is not perceived as community based is not community based regardless of its mission statement and plans. Members of the community must identify the institution as an educational resource for themselves or they will not use it. The National Center for Higher Education Management Systems has piloted systems for assessing the impact of community colleges on their communities and the case-study book (Lake, McClenney, and Gollattscheck, 1979) as well as other materials is available from the center. The community college that would strengthen its community-based operation would do well to begin by analyzing its image in the community.

Continuing education in community colleges may not exhibit all the characteristics of the "dependent unit of an organization whose main purpose is not continuing education of adults" discussed in Chapter One of this book. Nonetheless, many community college educators are concerned that community colleges have not always lived up to their past promises. Further, there is concern that future societal needs for lifelong learning will require institutions far more capable of providing such services than the average community college of today. Already many community colleges are involved in improving their readiness to meet such challenges. Several groups work with such institutions and publish materials which highlight model programs and are excellent resources for colleges wishing to develop better programs in continuing education. (The Center for Community Education at the American Association of Community and Junior Colleges publishes *Update/Interface;* the Cooperative for the Advancement of Community-Based Postsecondary Education publishes *Community-Based Programs That Work;* and the National Council on Community Services and Continuing Education publishes *Community Services CATALYST.*) There is room to invigorate community colleges to meet continuing education needs of today and tomorrow, and community colleges will need to continuously review their success in such an ever-growing, ever-changing endeavor.

References

Brawer, F. B. *Familiar Functions in New Containers: Classifying Community Education.* Topical Paper 71. Los Angeles: ERIC Clearinghouse for Junior Colleges, 1980.

Gleazer, E. J., Jr. *The Community College: Values, Vision, and Vitality.* Washington, D.C.: American Association of Community and Junior Colleges, 1980.

Gollattscheck, J. F., Harlacher, E. L., Roberts, E., and Wygal, B. R. *College Leadership for Community Renewal.* San Francisco: Jossey-Bass, 1976.

Lake, D. B., McClenney, B., and Gollattscheck, J. F. *Assessing Community—College Impacts: Three Case Studies.* Boulder, Colo.: National Center for Higher Education Management Systems, 1979.

Tadlock, M. "Planning: How to Get There." In E. L. Harlacher and J. F. Gollattscheck (Eds.), *New Directions for Community Colleges: Implementing Community-Based Education,* no. 21. San Francisco: Jossey-Bass, 1978.

James F. Gollattscheck is president of Valencia Community College in Orlando, Florida.

Since public school systems sponsor continuing education by choice, any strategy to build support must be pragmatic, realistic, and flexible.

Strengthening Public School Support for Continuing Education

Hal Beder

Public school continuing education programs vary across the United States: in some states federally funded (ABE) and high school-equivalency programs constitute the major or sole component of the public school programs, while in others learner fee-supported general enrichment and vocational programs predominate. Yet, regardless of the focus of the continuing education program, there are two characteristics of the relationships between public schools and their continuing education agencies that are important to an understanding of support. First, public schools are legally required to offer education to children and youth; they are not required to offer continuing education and do so only by choice. Second, by its very nature elementary and secondary education differs substantially from continuing education of adults. While children are a captive audience, adults are voluntary learners. While basic operating resources are given for public schools, continuing education programs have to generate most of their own resources. While public schools teach a predetermined curriculum designed to prepare youth for adult roles, continuing education offerings typically are responsive to the needs of adults. These characteristics make the support of the public school system particularly important, for if school systems do not support continuing education, vital resources may be reduced or the program eliminated. Furthermore, as Beder (1979) implies, because continuing education differs significantly from elementary and secondary education, unless school districts support continuing education to the extent that they are willing to grant sufficient autonomy to conduct programs in accordance with continuing education principles, the adult program may fail to function effectively.

If school system support for continuing education is important, at least two related questions are raised. First, what causes support, or the lack of it? Second, what strategies are effective for building and manifesting support? The answer to the first question is by no means conclusive. Mezirow, Darkenwald, and Knox (1975) suggest that community support for ABE is positively related to recruitment success, and Beder and Smith (1977) demonstrate that community support is related to ABE program growth. Beder (1979) reports a statistically significant relationship between the degree to which New Jersey public school systems and communities support their adult education programs and amount of operating autonomy. Beder also found that parent organization support was not related to the size of the continuing education program's enrollment or operating budget.

Lacking a comprehensive body of research germane to the specifics of public school system support for continuing education, it is logical to turn to practical experience and general theory in the behavioral sciences to develop an effective strategy for building support. Let us begin with several principles that are as basic as they are true. The main purposes of every organization are to attain organizational goals and to maintain organizational viability. Organizations support those activities that help them achieve their purposes, combat those influences inimical to their purposes, and adopt a neutral or indifferent position toward most other matters. From these principles the basic strategy for building sponsor system support is derived. Specifically, the continuing education agency should set goals that benefit the school system, achieve results that will be perceived as beneficial by the schools, and develop a fallback strategy should the first two steps fail. Let us examine these points in detail.

School System Benefit

In benefiting the public school system the continuing education agency should undertake activities that provide the greatest benefit to the school system while incurring the least amount of cost in the process. In the same regard, activities that cause the school system undue cost should be avoided. Or to put it more simply, the basic question is what can continuing education do that helps achieve important school system goals while minimizing problems for the schools.

Let us be more specific. Even though state and federal governments have exercised more and more control over school districts in recent years, the public schools still are community-based organizations dependent on community support. School administrators are well aware of this. Frequently, however, public schools are limited in their ability to garner support. As Litwak and Mayer (1966) note, schools tend to be large bureaucratic organizations that have difficulty dealing with smaller, more collegial community groups. Furthermore, the likeliest support base for most organizations rests among those who depend on the organization. This includes suppliers and recipients of service. Most suppliers of schools are external to the community, however, and the primary clients of public schools are school children and their parents. Although parent-teacher organizations, school sports activities, and the like are useful in creating support among client groups, a majority of a community's population is left out—the majority which has no school-age children. As coalitions of senior citizens and other community residents who do not have school-age children organize to defeat school budgets, administrators become well aware that they must court groups previously not reached by the schools.

Enter the continuing education program. By their very nature, continuing education programs serve a wide spectrum of adult taxpayers, unreached by any other school district service. Partially because they are highly dependent on the community for most resources, continuing education programs tend to form linkage relationships with a multitude of community organizations. For example, of two moderate-sized New York State public school ABE programs, one had formed student referral relationships with over thirty-six community organizations and the other had referral relationships with forty-two (Beder and Smith, 1977). In short, public school continuing education programs often maintain ongoing relations with a greater diversity of potential community support groups than the schools do, and typically these groups are the ones the public schools would like to influence but have difficulty in reaching. The obvious conclusion is that the continuing education program can greatly benefit the public schools by serving as a public relations organ to community groups in the public school's behalf and can, as we noted before, gain promoter support. There are countless ways of achieving this end; some examples tried elsewhere are: Make sure that all favorable publicity and advertising activities identify the continuing education program as an agency of the public schools. Promote the public schools in appearances before community groups and in meetings. Invite lay community leaders to attend adult program special events conducted in public school facilities. Make sure that public school officials are present and have high visibility in special activities open to the general public. Use clients as *common messengers* (Litwak and Mayer, 1966) by asking adult students to share with their families information the public schools desire to be disseminated. And finally, complaints about the public schools should be a private matter between continuing education administrators and public school officials. Problems that reflect negatively on the public schools should not be aired publicly.

In addition to assisting the public schools in a public relations capacity, continuing education programs are frequently able to be of budgetary assistance to public schools. Although elementary and secondary programs usually have much larger budgets than continuing education, the recent public press for accountability and general budgetary leanness has resulted in strict line-item accounting practices in most public schools. Each dollar is allocated to a predetermined purpose and there is little flexibility to make other purchases. Although budgetary practices vary, continuing education programs are sometimes able to share their purchases with regular elementary-secondary programs or to make small but greatly needed purchases for elementary-secondary use. For example, one public school continuing education agency purchased several microcomputers for use in personal computer programming courses. During the day, elementary-secondary students were encouraged to use the equipment. Other continuing education agencies have loaned or given typewriters, office equipment, cameras, and audio equipment to the schools for daytime use.

If purposefully benefiting the public schools is one side of the support coin, avoiding practices that interfere with public school operation and procedures is the other. This is not always easy. Just as the educational technology of elementary and secondary programs is affected by the need for student control and bureaucratic efficiency, the educational technology of continuing education programs is affected by the necessity of meeting the individually felt needs of clients. Adults are voluntary learners; unless instruction meets felt needs they will not participate and there will be no program. Moreover, learners are a requisite resource for adult programs, a resource which is not a given. Consequently, recruitment and retention are vital to continuing education in public schools and elsewhere.

The upshot is that while the policies and procedures of the schools necessarily are affected by the need for student control, continuing education programs generally want to stress flexibility and openness in meeting adult needs. While public schools adopt a managerial-bureaucratic operating style, continuing education tends to be more entrepreneurial. The contrast creates a situation ripe for intraorganizational conflict, conflict which can harm the weaker of the conflicting parties the most, and the weaker is nearly always continuing education.

Consequently, actions that disrupt or interfere with elementary-secondary operations should be avoided. Conflict may arise over facility use and scheduling. Mezirow, Darkenwald, and Knox (1975), for example, note that day-school teachers sometimes complain that evening adult activities leave their classrooms untidy. School business offices have been known to criticize continuing education directors for a failure to comply with standard procedures, and there are examples of conflict arising over parking regulations, insurance requirements, and prohibitions regarding food, alcohol, and smoking.

Communicate the Benefits

Quite obviously, all beneficial actions go for naught unless public school officials are aware of them and consider them to be beneficial. Thus, not only should the continuing education agency benefit the public schools if it is to enjoy support, but the continuing education agency should engage in some sound but generally subtle self-promotion. Promotion includes all purposeful efforts to communicate persuasively and, as with most communicative processes, the issues of what is communicated (the message) through what channels (the medium) to what effect is highly relevant. Persuasive messages may take several forms. One type includes messages that extol the quality of the continuing education effort. Accordingly, positive evaluation reports, favorable enrollment statistics, testimonials from satisfied learners, and communication from supportive community organizations should have wide circulation among public school personnel who count. In internal promotional efforts the human interest value of continuing education should not be ignored. Real-life examples of how educational activities have changed lives for the better have excellent public relations value internally as well as in the popular press. Finally, instances where continuing education has consciously undertaken efforts to benefit the schools should be brought to the attention of public school decision makers. For example, a continuing education agency that permitted the elementary-secondary program to use its equipment had the adult school logo stenciled on each piece in a conspicuous but not ostentatious fashion. The subtle message of benefit could not be ignored.

The channels available for internal promotion are generally obvious and include memos, reports, and appearances at meetings. Informal communication during the course of day-to-day interaction is especially effective and, obviously, conscious efforts to interact with elementary and secondary personnel facilitate information flow through all channels.

Adult learners can be a highly effective channel, for the veracity and seriousness of the message is seldom challenged when delivered through this source. Communication between satisfied learners and public school personnel should be encouraged.

Have a Fallback Strategy

No matter how much continuing education benefits the public schools and despite sophisticated efforts to promote the adult program, fate sometimes thwarts efforts to build support. A new and highly unsupportive superintendent or school board can wreak havoc. In budget crises, school officials have been known to eliminate continuing education even though adult programs cost school districts little or nothing. When the public school system unexpectedly withdraws support despite the continuing education agency's best efforts, a very difficult situation develops.

In most cases public school continuing education administrators are employees of the school system. If the directors are ordered by a superior to undertake actions harmful to their own program, they may have no choice but to accede; that is unless they have developed a fallback strategy for use as a last resort in such emergency situations. The critical element of such a fallback position is a power base independent of the school district which can exert influence on district officials in the agency's behalf. Coalitions of community organizations dependent on continuing education services can serve in this capacity, and continuing education offices located in state education departments have helped local agencies in disputes with their school districts in more than one case. An example involving an influential adult program advisory committee serves to illustrate the value of an independent power base.

In a certain large city public school continuing education program, a concert series was the mainstay of a cultural appreciation program and a major generator of revenue. Profits from the concerts were used to subsidize high-need, high-cost programs such as signing for the deaf. Tickets were sold out for a performance by a famous opera star. The morning of the performance the continuing education director received a call from the opera company's management. A singer had become ill, and the star in question had to fill in. He would not appear at the concert series.

The director was perplexed, for cancellation might undermine public confidence in the series with disastrous implications, so he reminded the opera company that he had a legal contract with the star and expected it to be honored. That was that—or so he thought. Shortly thereafter, the director received a second call, this time from the chancellor of the entire city school system. Cancel the program was the message, let the star sing at the opera that night.

Arguing with a chancellor is about as close to professional suicide as a director can come. Normally, the outlook would be dismal, but the director had cautiously developed his advisory board to serve as an advocacy body external to the school system. A call to an influential lawyer on the board resulted in an injunction prohibiting the star from singing at the opera that night. The injunction was gained in the name of the community and the director was thereby isolated from administrative reprisal.

The example has a happy ending. A compromise was struck so that the star was allowed to sing at the opera that evening, in return for two future concerts for the price of one.

In conclusion, it is safe to say that support of the school district is a vital issue for continuing education. This is true for two reasons. First, public school districts sponsor continuing education by choice; when there is no support, the adult program is in extreme jeopardy. Second, differences between the manner in which elementary-secondary schools operate and the way continuing education programs operate create the potential for conflict between the adult program and the parent organization, conflict which must be avoided if support is to be enjoyed.

Given the necessity of public school system support, a strategy is needed to build and maintain it. One viable strategy is based on three practical principles. First, undertake actions beneficial to the school district whenever possible; second, promote the continuing education agency with the public school system so that actions will be perceived as beneficial; and third, build a base of influence independent of the school system that can be used in continuing education's behalf as a last resort.

References

Beder, H. W. "The Relationship of Community and Sponsor System Support to Selected Aspects of Adult Education Agency Functioning." *Adult Education,* 1979, *19* (2), 96-108.

Beder, H. W., and Smith, F. *Developing an Adult Education Program Through Community Linkages.* Washington, D.C.: Adult Education Association of the U.S.A., 1977.

Litwak, E., and Mayer, H. "A Balance Theory of Coordination Between Bureaucratic Organizations and Community Primary Gaps." *Administrative Science Quarterly.* 1966, *11*, 31-58.

Mezirow, J., Darkenwald, G., and Knox, A. *Last Gamble on Education.* Washington, D.C.: Adult Education Association of the U.S.A., 1975.

Hal Beder is an associate professor of adult education at Rutgers University and codirector of the Center for Adult Development.

Educational programs for older adults will enhance any educational program, adding a constituency that will support the adult school, provide it with new challenges, and give it an intergenerational student body.

Establishing Public School Programs for Older Adults

Marion G. Marshall

In 1961, the education section of the White House Conference on Aging declared:

> As a Nation we realize that continued planning and preparation are needed to ensure the well being, the strength, and the happiness of the older adult, his family, and his society. People need to prepare through continuing education as they prepare for earlier periods of life. . . . There must be coordinated efforts among all agencies involved in education of older people [U.S. Senate . . ., 1961, p. 7].

There are 34 million people over the age of sixty in this country. The United States Office of Education has said, "Because older Americans are increasing faster than any other segment of the population, educational programs that attend to their special needs are spreading like crab grass" (Fricke, 1979, p. 1). Crab-grass growth, however, is not the ideal. What is needed are systematic, purposeful programs that encourage people to continue learning, and that allow for individual differences and desires.

Education has been, and continues to be, one of the most talked about, praised, and maligned areas of living. It has long been recognized that a well-educated populace will help make a strong, effective country. Therefore, everyone has ideas on how education should be administered, who should be allowed to be educated, what such learning should cost, and where and how to teach. Seldom are older people an important group in these considerations. The growth in numbers of senior citizens points to a fact that they can no longer be ignored. Education for older adults must now be considered an equal segment of lifelong educational plans and processes.

As part of a secondary or unified school district, continuing education units come under the jurisdiction of departments of education in the various states. Thus, they are guided by state laws and funding regulations. Emphasis in these departments is generally placed on children who must attend school until they have reached a certain age—generally sixteen years. Adding continuing education broadens thinking, planning, and acceptance of its value and need. When these concepts are expanded to include older adults—55 years of age and over—still further expansion of thinking and use of funds must be accepted.

In 1948, Los Angeles City Schools' older-adult programming began when one adult school principal noted older people sitting on a bus bench discussing an issue of current importance. There was not enough room on the bench to accommodate them all, so the principal invited them into the school. He asked if they would like to meet regularly, saying he would be pleased to offer them space and, if they liked, a teacher. The group responded positively, notices were distributed throughout the community, and within a month a second class had to be started. So the program grew. Today, Los Angeles adult schools offer some 300 classes to older adults throughout the city.

Not all classes began so easily. During the beginning years of the Title I "Poverty Program," funds were received to try to develop classes in two poverty areas. It took six months to get enough students to maintain classes. But today, because the school district persisted, these areas boast large groups of older adults, hundreds of whom are faithful students. Some have pursued high school diplomas, but most are interested in discussions and skills classes. They enjoy the companionship as well as the mental and physical stimulation.

Establishing a Program

How, then, does a public school establish classes for older adults? First, a determination of need must be established. It is anticipated that one in five Americans will be over the age of sixty in the year 2000, and that this figure will rise to one in four by the year 2030. At the same time, the numbers of young adults will be lower. Therefore, schools and colleges will be looking for more students to compensate for declining enrollments. Older adults, at the same time, will be more demanding of educational institutions than they are now. They will have more leisure time and be healthier and better educated. They will expect that programs available for them will be stimulating, both mentally and physically.

Recognizing these national trends is helpful, but it is essential to localize an assessment, for each area is unique and must be considered as such.

There are many ways to do a needs analysis. News articles, especially in local shoppers' newspapers; flyers distributed in the community; and meetings of key groups of older people and agencies serving them are all possible. The latter method is often slower, but more thorough and more representative of a total community involvement.

Experience points strongly to the fact that decision makers—those administrators, legislators, and board members who control the activities allowed—must be sold on the values and needs for continuing education for older community residents. Community support may be the most important factor in successful organization and programming.

Once this is done, an advisory committee of community older adults is in order. Include on this committee older adults who are leaders, for leadership is far more important in such planning than is the previous level of educational achievement of the individuals.

Plans must be made with the committee for ways to reach all ages of people in the area. Often younger people urge older persons to attend school. Use the committee members as sounding boards, to go into the community to talk with residents, to give information, to determine the kind of classes that will be best, to establish budgets, and even to help find funding for the new program.

Berridge (1978, p. 18-19) outlines steps for successful initiation of a program. Those steps appropriate to this study are: "Securing a commitment from the superintendent and board of education . . . appointing a steering committee to assist in planning the project . . . developing and finalizing a working budget . . . and . . . fully informing the community of the process and its potential through news media, films, and special purpose meetings."

Berridge's seventh step (p. 18) is "informing and seeking assistance from all identifiable groups, organizations, agencies, and institutions, through a group meeting; holding a follow-up meeting to ascertain their commitments and to form a coordinating board." Let us dwell on this point again. Older-adult services are available in this country through federal, state, and local agencies. Social Security, the Administration on Aging, state departments on aging, ACTION, clubs and federation of older adults, welfare agencies, and many religious organizations offer programs. At the same time, public schools provide educational services to children and adults. Together, these groups can offer strong, workable older-adult programs.

Berridge advocates the employment of a full-time coordinator to be in charge of the project and represent the school at advisory committee and board meetings. The 1971 White House Conference on Aging went further. The education section adopted a recommendation that each state appoint an older-adult specialist in its education department. Yet, as of this date, only California has done so! Most of California's 322 adult schools have programs designed for and primarily attended by senior citizens. This would not be possible without professional time and energy made available to those schools desiring to serve older residents. This points clearly to the fact that having a recommendation may not be enough. Strong advocacy is needed to make the recommendation become reality.

Coordinating Efforts

Recreation departments, therapy programs, and educational programs need to clear with each other to be certain that there is no *unnecessary* duplication. Please note the word unnecessary. Too often agencies and organizations worry about duplication of efforts, when no one group can possibly serve everyone. For example, the local adult school may offer academic studies, arts and fine art, and group discussions that keep older adults abreast of the times. Community colleges may offer paraprofessional training and many of the same classes as the adult schools, but for a segment of the population that is more comfortable in a campus setting. The university may give professional training to gerontologists and other professionals involved in serving older people. All of these institutions also can avail themselves of the peer teaching, tutoring, and other services that seniors may offer as volunteers or aides. Such intergenerational contacts may be serendipitous but should be encouraged. People of all ages, learning and working together, help make an educational institution strong.

What about classrooms? Many older people enjoy having their own classes, where they can interact with people their own ages. But these need not be rooms in school buildings. Rather, they can be held in places older people gather, such as senior centers, churches or synagogues, park buildings, retirement homes, or nursing facilities.

There will be some older people who prefer traditional campus rooms, where they can mix with young students and feel the stimulation of competition with them. Here is one place that your advisory committee is most useful, for part of the assessment of need and interest can help decide how many, and in what areas of study, people will attend classes.

Outreach is a recent concept of educational approach; yet because it is practical and productive, the practice of outreach has developed rapidly. The National Advisory Council on Adult Education (1980, p. 16) defines *outreach* as "activities designed to (i) inform adult populations who are least educated and most in need of assistance of the availability and benefits of the adult education program; and (ii) assist those adult populations to participate in the program by providing reasonable and convenient access."

For the purposes of most programs for older adults, the definition is most appropriate. The second part should be carefully noted. Many older adults would like to attend school if there were a way to get to classes. Agencies should provide transportation or escort services.

If access to a room is too difficult for older people suffering handicapping conditions, a ramp or better lighting may make the difference. These adjustments can be made to accommodate most people. Here again, agency cooperation and support of the local school district is important.

One strategy for assuring success is to educate older-adult community leaders in the ways of board of education meetings. Have them attend board meetings regularly and make their presence known to the board members, and their wishes will be considered more seriously.

In California when elimination of the older-adult programs from public school funding was threatened following passage of Proposition 13, groups of older students jammed board rooms, demanding that their classes be continued. Though they didn't win all that they wanted, the state program was continued. In spite of cutbacks, some programs even started where none had existed before.

Gaining Support

Convincing peers and colleagues is often essential in providing a program for older adults. Mention old people, and someone in the group will make a remark intended as humor. It is usually derogatory, often pointed at an individual in the group.

It may take just one successful event to prove the values of lifelong education. An example: A staff meeting was disrupted when one member suggested a conference on Death and Dying. After a brief shock, members began talking about "the obvious fact that it won't work. Old people don't want to talk about death." However, no one wanted to stop talking about the subject! When this was pointed out, acceptance was immediate and unanimous. The conference was a success. After that, the district wholeheartedly supported older-adult education.

Another example is provided by a 1970 Los Angeles United Way Survey. Professional people representing many service agencies put education for older people at the bottom of a long list of needs. Older people, using the same list, put education fifth—topped only by income maintenance, housing, health, and transportation.

When decision makers point to the expense of a program for older people, remind them that it is far less costly to keep people occupied, productive, and healthy than to pay for hospitalization due to mental or physical illness.

Taking key members of a staff, board members, and other community leaders to observe a class of older adults may prove the values of the program. The enthusiasm of the older students, and of the teacher, can convince even the most skeptical. Recently, a sixty-four-year-old woman earned her high school diploma and was selected, because of her popularity with the students and her devotion to education, as a graduation speaker. She urged everyone, "Do what I did... you can be educated at any age, and you can get that dream of yours." Hearing this, a board member whispered to the principal, "Everybody should hear Maxine, then we'd have programs for older people throughout the nation."

Locating a funding source for a particular project can boost the possibilities of instituting such a program. The project may involve classes in the humanities, such as those designed by the National Council on Aging. It may involve education for new careers, paid or volunteer, and be funded by the state employment development department, or the agency on aging. Local foundations often give money to offer classes in special places, such as nursing homes or churches, or in special areas of study. It may be possible to "latch on" to an ongoing program of nutrition or exercise. State departments of aging, community education programs, or national foundations often invite proposals for projects. Money received is usually for "seed" or for demonstration ideas that can be replicated. Canvass colleagues and the community for ideas. This frequently generates interest as well as new ideas and continuing support.

The 1979 revision of Title V of the Education Act lists older adults as among the "least educated, most in need" groups that are to have priority in continuing education. This chapter has suggested ways in which public school support for the education of older adults can be enhanced. If it is agreed that education is a lifelong process and the right of all individuals, then older adults should be included in all educational programs for adults. Such movement will help the learning society to flourish!

References

Berridge, R. I. *The Community Education Handbook*. Midland, Mich.: Pendell, 1978.

Fricke, N. W. "Education and Fulfillment of Need for Older Adults." Unpublished thesis, California State University, Sacramento, 1979.

National Advisory Council on Adult Education. *Terms, Definitions, Organizations, and Councils Associated with Adult Learning*. Washington, D.C.: Superintendent of Documents, 1980.

U.S. Senate Special Committee on Aging. *The 1961 White House Conference on Aging—Basic Policy Statements and Recommendations*. Washington, D.C.: U.S. Government Printing Office, 1961.

Marion Marshall is currently consultant in programs for older adults for the California State Department of Education. She has previously been gerontology specialist in the Division of Career and Continuing Education, Los Angeles Unified School District, and a parent-educator and gerontology teacher in the classroom and on television for the Los Angeles Unified School District.

By increasing their involvement in continuing education, public libraries can strengthen public support and help insure their own survival.

Continuing Education in Libraries: A Challenge to Change Agents

Barbara Conroy

From its inception, the library has been a source of information and learning. The campus or school library supports the educational role of its institution. The special library serves its agency, business, or industry with specialized information geared to the organization's function. The public library, rather than being supported as the information-education unit of a defined organization, seeks to serve similar purposes for its community and its society.

For a public library, the tasks of defining its role, understanding the needs of its public, and extending services to users rests substantially on initiative and leadership shown by the library itself. Particularly in the United States, service patterns are shaped by individual libraries and by the expectations of the community and the larger society. The extent to which those patterns involve continuing education depends on beliefs and behaviors of library staff and decision makers, library traditions and resources, and community pressures.

Meeting adult learners' needs has long been a defined role of the public library. Broad endorsement exists for libraries to provide opportunities and to encourage people to educate themselves continuously. Landmark studies (Knight and Nourse, 1969; Leigh, 1950; Martin, 1972) repeatedly identify this as a primary library goal. Recently, lay people met with librarians to rank lifelong learning as one of five major national conference topics and to recommend it as a central effort of libraries (National Commission on Libraries . . . , 1980). Thus, history indicates both a past and present commitment to continuing education.

To some extent, libraries' activities also reflect learning as an accepted role as well as a stated commitment. Informally, many libraries support the educational efforts of other organizations with materials, facilities, or special services. Linkages are made with community education efforts, free universities, and adult basic education programs. Classes and discussion groups may be library sponsored and backed with library resources. For example, a few libraries offer literacy classes; some are active brokers for educational information; many are involved with Great Books programs. Assisting the adult independent learner has long been a standard library service through reference, interlibrary loan, and bibliographies. Certainly normal functions of selecting, organizing, and disseminating information and materials serve the educational pursuits of individuals and groups. In some libraries, adult services is a structural unit designated to coordinate educational services.

But, for the most part, only scattered examples of public library support of continuing education exist, many fewer than might be expected in view of the library's stated purpose. Continuing education is not at present a major component of standard library service. Nor is it a consistently accepted work unit with assigned staffing and coordinative functions. Most often, outside funding sources such as foundations, the Office of Education, or the National Endowment for the Humanities initiate those continuing education programs that do exist. And, regrettably, such programs often do not survive beyond the funded period.

Thus, in some libraries, increased support is needed to initiate continuing education efforts. In others, support must be sought to improve and extend present efforts. Strategy for gaining the support must concentrate on the broader community and the entire library field, as well as upon the staffs in individual libraries. To be credible, the change message must persuade library decision makers that continuing education is legitimate, viable, and beneficial. Strategies are needed to convince those not yet active and to sustain those active but struggling with budget or belief barriers. Strategies that institutionalize continuing education efforts through policies and programs are necessary to move spoken commitment to action.

Two Change Projects

Two efforts have led individual public libraries and the library profession toward an identifiable continuing education function. Each reveals important links between continuing education and libraries. As examples, each serves to illustrate how a national program can affect local service patterns, redirect professional vision, and nudge a tradition-bound field. Finally, even this brief review may reveal some elements vital to the process of change.

The tremendous growth of the continuing education movement and the close relationship between libraries and the movement was a leading influence in pushing library service beyond bookroom walls. In the 1950s the Fund for Adult Education reflected this relationship and inspired cooperation. Funded by the Ford Foundation through the American Library Association, six projects worked together to spark continuing education efforts in libraries:

1. The survey of Adult Education in Public Libraries provided a foundation for planning and research and gave an excellent profile of the library's educational role.

2. The Library Community Project identified long-term continuing education needs on the basis of community needs analyses in eight states plus publications and consultant services.

3. The American Heritage Project focused on issue-oriented discussion programs through local libraries using library staff as discussion leaders and coordinators.

4. The Subgrant Project prompted, through funding, new and expanded continuing education projects in local libraries which revealed the importance of libraries as a valuable means of delivery.

5. The Allerton Park Librarian Training Conference identified skills needed by librarians for continuing education tasks and provided materials and training.

6. The Office for Adult Education performed coordinative functions for these five projects and granted discretionary funding for additional smaller projects.

An evaluation concluded that the effort "produced more skilled professionals, stronger adult education institutions, and a profession better able to define its role in adult education and more willing to accept the responsibilities in the total adult education field" (Hewitt, 1958, p. 178).

In retrospect, several useful change strategies can be noted. The reasoned approach over nearly ten years made substantial impact on changing concepts of library service and on the evolving relationship between continuing education and libraries. Several forces worked together to produce this impact. Specific projects demonstrated the rationale's validity; definite leadership and specific funding sustained the effort, as well as initiated it; involvement and special training convinced and prepared practitioners; and national diffusion of projects and information made change possible. Nonetheless, though this effort was significant in promoting new service concepts and moving the field philosophically, it was insufficient to securely integrate these practices into standard library service or to sustain the close relationships between continuing education and librarianship begun during that period. It did, however, furnish an important breakthrough and a foundation for subsequent efforts.

A second effort has been a deliberate attempt to move libraries toward a more active and supportive role to provide substantial services to self-directed learners. Most certainly these efforts in the mid 1970s benefited from the foundation laid by the earlier effort. The Adult Independent Learning Project selected the public library "because it represents a major information resource in the community and because its primary function is to serve the community as an information center" (Mavor, Toro, and DeProspo, 1976, Part I, p. 2).

The project identified two kinds of help important to independent learners: advisory services and information support services. Each extended traditional library reference service to involve extensive interaction between a librarian and a learner; and each entailed developing a learning plan, then identifying and selecting resources from library and community to implement it. The librarian became an active link, at times an advocate, between the learner and needed resources.

From 1972 to 1976, this project sought to promote and perpetuate library acceptance and support of this continuing education function and role. By its own report, efforts to bring about "planned change in the current practices of public library service to adult independent learners required the application of a conscious and deliberate strategy of dissemination and the creation of a structure that would persist over time for guiding and implementing this strategy" (Mavo, Toro, and DeProspo, 1976, Part II, p. 67).

The project provided several opportunities for in-process evaluation and assessment. Before it was launched, the College Entrance Examination Board (CEEB) tested the feasibility of a library-based information service for adults seeking college credit by examination. A CEEB Office of Library Independent Study and Guidance Projects was created to administer this project. Jointly funded by the Council on Library Resources, National Endowment for the Humanities, U.S. Office of Education, and the CEEB, the project worked initially with nine demonstration libraries. It identified and described services for adult independent learners, promoted public library interest in more active work with adult learners, provided staff training, assisted with testing and evaluation of services, and disseminated information about the project's broader significance as well as its specific activities and accomplishments.

Outcomes from this project include: active Learners Advisory Services (or variations thereof) in several public libraries, a model for establishing adult learner services, evaluative information useful for making decisions and for accountability. An additional outcome reveals the broad concept of this project. A Consortium for Public Library Innovation was formed and some of the original demonstration libraries were included to share with each other what had been learned. Prototype development and research was a focus. However, the consortium disbanded in June 1980.

In addition to the project itself and its outcomes, the description of the process is valuable to those interested in organizational change in public service organizations. Looking at change itself, the project identified certain factors concerning public libraries in particular, and likely in other types of service organizations, that should be considered in a change strategy (Mavor, Toro, and DeProspo, 1976, Part II, pp. 67-68).

> First, the present allocation of funds to the various interests and departments within a public library often conflicts with the alternative uses of these interests and departments. Second, the Learners Advisory Service has generated additional threats to the morale of professionals who are comfortable with existing practices and a segmented departmentalized approach to service and clients. Third, the manner in which planning and evaluation is presently carried out (in libraries) typically does not provide an avenue for introducing innovations. Current library practices focus on acquiring, organizing, and preserving collections of materials. . . . Models to effect changes in the delivery of a responsive service to the individual are frequently hampered by a preoccupation with this function of warehousing and the provision of a mass service through brief reference interviews. . . . Fourth, organizational problems in the public library identify communications difficulties and role conflicts at points of exchange (between the learner and librarian). The question of who talks to whom in disseminating the innovation and the roles that are assumed in the exchange demand a more direct approach that goes beyond merely providing information on the achievements of a given project.

The project also reported conditions apparently needed for success in this change effort as: active support of top administration, extensive involvement of facilities and staff providing the service, establishment of a personnel system of recognition and reward for desirable performance, and careful monitoring to assure that new procedures are not rejected or ignored by staff. With hindsight, we can see that each of these factors are probably relevant to the earlier action supported by the Fund for Adult Education.

These two efforts, the earlier project supported by the Fund for Adult Education and the more recent Adult Independent Learning Project, attempted and, to some extent, managed to change the level and nature of continuing education activity in public libraries. The first expanded services to adult learners beyond library facilities. The second deepened the interchange between librarian and library user. Each emphasized the library as part of the community.

Each dealt with problems associated with initiating new services, role definitions, internal resistance, and the need for means to sustain the changes once they had been initiated. Each worked with libraries throughout the country, both as a means to demonstrate the feasibility of what was being proposed and as a means to channel innovation a number of ways. Each identified and used leadership resources both from the library and from continuing education, often strengthening library staff with additional training for the change.

Each was made possible through funding sources outside the library field, although substantial contributions were also made on the part of the participating libraries. Each used several means of involvement to build investment and ownership both in the activities and in the outcomes. Each tried to sustain and continue the change effort although they used different methods. The Fund for Adult Education stretched out the effort over an extended period. The Adult Independent Learning Project evolved an additional effort to include a broader focus and new participant libraries. Both increased the level of support for continuing education in public libraries in two ways: each brought a new emphasis on continuing education in specific libraries using a conscious change process and each disseminated the innovation to impact libraries in general.

Future Directions

What, then, is the message for the next generation of change agents seeking to increase support for continuing education in libraries? Three factors are important to any new effort to increase such support. The first is that the public library now faces challenges to its survival. Rapid technological change in an information-oriented society requires review and redefinition of the library's role. Tightening public budgets, inflationary costs, and increased competition from other information service providers further restricts resources for new programs. This confrontation may elicit two different responses depending on how it is perceived and used. One response is to paralyze library decision makers with fear, preventing intensified continuing education efforts. Or, it may convince librarians that continuing education is a partial, but important, answer to the survival issue. Since continuing education meets an increasing community demand, expanded library service is already seen as a basis for community support for the library.

Second, those seeking to gain support for continuing education in libraries will again look toward funding external to libraries. Current emphasis on lifelong learning includes public and private funding sources. The competition for these funds is intense and may drive a wedge between continuing educators and librarians as was done in the two efforts described here.

A third factor should also be considered. Though some conceptual impact was made on library goals by the Fund's efforts and the Adult Independent Learning Project brought change in several libraries and resulted in a Consortium for Public Library Innovation, there has been no major change in basic public library services offered in most communities. Libraries do not have wide support from opinion leaders or those who allocate public and private funds. Neither is there within libraries a sufficient critical mass of individuals able to effect change.

Perhaps the most significant conclusion to be drawn from an examination of the two change efforts described here is that those seeking to increase the library's role in continuing education at this point should try another way. Estabrook (1979, p. 151) asserts that "one can only conclude that there has been little systemic change" in terms of community library services as a result of support for some fifteen years from the Library Services and Construction Act.

The change message, though heard by some, was missed by most. Perhaps it was heard but did not convince. Unfortunately, very little change has occurred beyond those libraries that were part of the funded projects. Not all the blame for failure to change can rest with the lack of resources. Part of hearing a change message is to obtain the resources. With sufficient conviction and commitment, resources can be found.

Changes in libraries are vital and urgent. The direction of sound change is most likely to be in the area of expansion of library roles and functions in continuing education. Libraries have proved neutrality in sponsorship and distribution of information, materials, and services. This is not always the case in organizations such as academe, government, and business and industry, which sometimes emphasize their own needs and priorities (biases) rather than openly seeing the priorities and needs of the learner. In face of increasing competition for informational and educational services, a convincing case might well be made for increasing support for continuing education through libraries as a viable response to the issue of public library survival.

References

Estabrook. "Emerging Trends in Community Library Services." In M. Monroe and K. Heim (Eds.), *Library Trends*, 1979, *28* (2), 151-163.

Hewitt, C. H. *Grant Evaluation Study*. Chicago: American Library Association, 1958.

Knight, D. M., and Nourse, E. S. (Eds.). *Libraries at Large*. New York: Bowker, 1969.

Leigh, D. *The Public Library in the United States: The General Report of the Public Library Inquiry*. New York: Columbia University Press, 1950.

Martin, A. B. *A Strategy for Public Library Change: Proposed Public Library Goals—Feasibility Study*. Chicago: American Library Association, 1972.

Mavor, A. S., Toro, J. O., and DeProspo, E. R. *Final Report. The Role of the Public*

Libraries in Adult Independent Learning. Parts I and II. New York: College Entrance Examination Board, 1976.

National Commission on Libraries and Information Science. *The White House Conference on Library and Information Services—1979: The Final Report, Summary.* Washington, D.C.: National Commission on Libraries and Information Science, 1980.

Barbara Conroy is an educational consultant who works with libraries, library associations, graduate library schools, and state library agencies. She has directed projects on continuing education and libraries, including a Task Force of the Adult Education Association.

Consolidation has proved itself effective in strengthening one company's corporate training and education program.

Strengthening Corporate Continuing Education: A Case History

Martin E. Smith

The case for improving effectiveness of training and education activities can be made by describing one company's efforts. These employee education efforts were directed at consolidating resources and managing them more efficiently. The issue at stake was: Are corporate training and education needs better served by one large training department or by many small training staffs directly controlled by the departments?

Traditionally, corporate officers had considered decentralized training and education to be more responsive to departmental needs and better integrated with other staff services, such as the publication of methods documentation. Thus, in 1977 the company had twenty-nine training staffs with 495 full- and part-time personnel. An incomplete attempt to centralize training in the early '70s had grouped 26 percent of the continuing education program administrators into a corporate staff.

Weaknesses of this early plan were little or no accounting of training volume (participants or participant days), staff size, cost, quality, efficiency, or future demands. Furthermore, continuing education and training faced rapidly expanding demands because of (1) growing competition in telecommunications, which stimulated new products, services, and expansion of the sales force; (2) automation of many work operations, which led to radical redesign of jobs and movement of employees from shrinking to stable or expanding job categories; and (3) retirement of the many employees hired shortly after World War II.

Because of these trends, efforts to consolidate continuing education and training were renewed in 1977. The advantages claimed for centralization included more effective control of costs and quality, more flexible and efficient use of resources (people, budgets, facilities), and the opportunity to develop expertise in critical functions, such as organizational planning. The question was how to achieve these benefits without sacrificing responsiveness and integration with other staff services.

Reorganization

For convenience, the reorganization process may be divided into five stages. This is a post hoc interpretation. There was no masterplan, even though there was an overall goal. Planning proceeded one stage at a time.

The initiative came from the corporate staff. Planning activities were distributed across four levels of management. Senior managers set goals and priorities, reviewed and approved specific plans, and negotiated with corporate executives for support. Middle and junior managers performed the detailed design work and administrative tasks.

Stage 1: Awareness. In early 1977, the manager of the corporate education and training staff advocated the consolidation of training. Upper management rejected the proposal as too radical. Instead, the vice-presidents' council was petitioned to authorize a study of the quality and cost of corporate education and training. The vice-presidents appointed two ad hoc groups: a task force of middle managers, including educators and line managers, to do the work, and a steering committee of assistant vice-presidents to evaluate the findings.

Stage 2: Investigations. The task force found (1) training costs much higher than anticipated, (2) many course design faults, (3) projections of sharp increases in training volume, and (4) no standard procedure for cost accounting, quality control, and forecasting (Chellino, Rice, and Dinneen, 1978). The task force recommended (1) an expense tracking system, (2) standardized course development procedures, (3) quality control procedures, and (4) long-range forecasting of demand for continuing education training. These recommendations were approved by the steering committee and the executive council in September 1977. A second task force was commissioned to design the recommended procedures. The steering committee was charged with monitoring the next phase.

Stage 3: Administrative Systems. The recommendations were translated into four plans which were approved by the two committees and instituted in January 1979. A task force was converted into a permanent staff to administer these plans, which are described briefly in the following paragraphs.

The Quarterly Report System is a process for compiling statistics about education and training operations, including volume by course, function (development, delivery), facility, and client organization (trainee expenses); efficiency indexes for instructor and facility use; and project status of courses under development. These reports serve several purposes: input to forecasting, detection of problems which may trigger investigation through an operational review, and a historical data base for establishing group performance standards.

Second is the Long-Range Forecasting Plan, which looks ahead five years to training facilities and staff. The plan uses historical data, seat requests for the next scheduling cycle, training managers' estimates of future demand, project status report for courses under development, work force projections, and the educational implications of future corporate plans, products, and systems.

Local and Abridged Training Development Standards measures the course development process. This document defines the steps to be followed and how to document them. The development process involves seven phases: problem analysis, task analysis, course design, materials preparation, classroom try-out, distribution, and follow-up evaluation. By corporate policy, course developers must adhere to these standards or to a more comprehensive set published by AT&T (Shoemaker, 1979).

Finally, the Training Management Operational Review Plan (Smith, 1979, 1980) is designed to evaluate activities of a training and education staff. The plan provides directions, instruments, and summary forms for twenty-two data-collection exercises which measure thirty-five variables. An extensive review may include classroom observations, job observations of recent graduates, analyses of test data, interviews with graduates and their supervisors, and interviews with instructors and their supervisors. The review may take up to three months but yields a detailed report of staff strengths and weaknesses as well as recommendations for remedial action.

Stage 4: Reorganization. In April 1979, the vice-president's council was approached with a proposal to consolidate training staffs into one department. To support the proposal, quarterly report data were presented to show dramatic growth in training volume (student days up 33 percent) and cost (up 28 percent) between 1976 (reported by the first task force) and 1979 (projected from first-quarter results). The first four operational reviews suggested widespread problems, including instructors receiving no feedback on their teaching performance, obsolete and marginally relevant course content, trainees' proficiency not measured in the course, recent graduates unable to perform a critical task, principal parts of the job not covered in training, and basic content variations between different instructors of the same course. The vice-president's council approved consolidation.

Over the next eighteen months, training staffs were gradually merged. The transfers of people and budgets were negotiated to avoid disruption of training activities. To allay concerns about responsiveness to departmental needs and coordination with other staff services, curriculum committees were established in various job specialties. These committees included representatives of line organizations which send employees to training and of staff groups which decide the work methods upon which course content depends. These committees meet several times a year to discuss development priorities and scheduling issues. In one specialty, training and methods managers worked out a set of guidelines for coordinating training with the publication of new work methods. Training managers were also concerned about the limits of their responsibility and authority. To mitigate these concerns, managers of the merged staffs were delegated as committees to design their own organization, in other words, to allocate responsibilities and personnel among groups.

Stage 5: Program Changes. Consolidation facilitated policy and program changes. Some of the significant changes that occurred during or shortly after reorganization are described in the following paragraphs.

A lengthy (about forty-five days), high-volume (about one hundred twenty-five trainees per year) curriculum was redesigned. Changes included update and standardization of course content; converting from small group (two to four participants per class) to self-paced format (average of six participants per instructor); standardization of test materials and procedures; more realistic simulation of customer contacts by using full-time role players; many more practice exercises; audiotaping of exercises and tests for more effective feedback. Preliminary evaluation data indicated that graduates attained self-sufficiency on the job quicker than graduates of the original course. At the same time, the redesign reduced average time for education by ten days and eliminated twenty-five instructor positions.

Comprehensive curriculums were specified for many more job titles and specialties within job titles. These specifications defined required and optional courses, their sequence, and optimal timing expressed as intervals from appointment to job title.

An instructor certification plan was implemented to assure preparation of new instructors. The plan included requirements for basic instructor training and mandatory supervisory evaluations (based on classroom observations) of new instructors.

Two courses were added to the curriculum for course development personnel. One was introductory, based upon the local development standards. The second was a project manager's workshop which taught such tasks as evaluating the job performance of course developers, project planning, and reviewing draft instructional materials.

A new measurement plan for evaluating staff performance was introduced. The plan includes a survey of recent course graduates and their supervisors. The survey elicits judgments about course relevance and the graduate's job proficiency.

Planning studies have become common. Two noteworthy examples were a study of the cost and capacity of each training facility and a study to measure training costs more precisely.

Conditions and Strategies

The goal of consolidation has been achieved. Over 80 percent of training personnel work in the education and training department. And, there is ample evidence of administrative and instructional improvements. Staffing levels have been stabilized. A management information system has been implemented. Quality control procedures have been instituted. Instructional innovation has been accelerated. Efforts have been made to upgrade the professional proficiency of the continuing educators. Planning and forecasting studies are now recurring activities.

A case history, such as this report, does not permit cause-and-effect conclusions. Nevertheless, we can point to salient features of the change process and speculate about the critical factors. For discussion, these features have been divided into two categories: conditions and strategy.

As noted earlier, consolidation had been proposed and rejected in the early 1970s. In contrast to the earlier occasion, several conditions had changed. Economic and technological factors had stimulated training. Volume, staff size, and costs were proliferating. As a consequence, training assumed greater importance and was now widely seen as a separate function requiring tighter control.

Concurrently, centralized administration became more accepted in business and industry (Bowser, 1977; Moore and Kondrasuk, 1976). In fact, a private survey in 1978 showed that ten of twenty telecommunications companies had consolidated most of their education and training efforts. Consequently, consolidation was now seen as a possibility to be considered.

In 1979, the company underwent a massive reorganization (Behind AT&T's Change..., 1979) that put several training staffs in organizations different from some of their traditional client groups. Consolidation could provide a neutral ground for ensuring equal access to educational services for all client groups.

As a final condition, the earlier attempt at consolidation had left a small corporate staff that became the cadre for the current effort.

The change strategy evolved over several years. While the objective was clear from the start, planning proceeded one phase at a time, in three-to-twelve-month intervals. As a consequence, tactics were mixed. For example, in stage 2, a problem-analysis approach (Rummler, 1972) was used. In stage 3, the Quarterly Report System was designed according to systems development methodology (Kirk, 1973). Aspects of phase 4 were modeled after an organizational design process (Maher, 1979). I think this eclectic approach represented a responsiveness to the changing demands of the project.

It is difficult to identify exactly which factors won executive support for reorganization. A great deal of effort went into maintaining credibility. It was felt that the decision makers' perceptions of the change process was as important as the validity of the problem analysis, or the logic of the organizational design. Credibility was developed through extensive use of data and a step-by-step incremental change process.

Whenever the vice-president's council was approached, data were presented: data to illustrate a problem, data to show the results from implementing a prior decision. Even in the first stage, the petition to investigate training was supported with illustrative data. In stage 3, priority was given to developing the information system and the evaluation process which produced the critical data for the reorganization decision.

The gradual step-by-step process seemed less radical or threatening than consolidation itself. Each phase was a logical progression from the prior phase, and eventually all concerned came to accept the inevitability of consolidation. The gradual approach also avoided the pitfall of taking on more responsibility than could be handled at any one time. A breakdown in educational services would have aborted the change process.

Another strategic concern was the inclusion of various interest groups in decision-making and design activities. Executives representing the client organizations served on a committee which monitored the investigation and design teams. Field and methods managers currently serve on curriculum boards that represent the concerns of the client organizations. Managers incorporated into the training department were allowed to design major parts of the new organization.

The preceding discussion describes the application of planned change strategies to education and training programs in a large corporation. In terms of administrative and educational innovations, this effort was successful. The more important question of whether the company has benefited by these innovations is currently being evaluated. In retrospect, success may be attributed to the following factors: timing the change to take advantage of favorable conditions, the skills and determination of a small cadre, use of data to support decisions, patience, and inclusion of stakeholders in decision-making and design activities.

References

"Behind AT&T's Change at the Top." *Businessweek*, November 6, 1979, pp. 115–123.

Bowser, R. D. "Should I Try to Centralize Training in My Company?" *Training*, 1977, *14* (11), 39-40.

Chellino, S. N., Rice, R. L., and Dinneen, M. "A Corporate Training Audit." Paper presented at annual meetings of the National Society for Performance and Instruction, San Francisco, March 24, 1978.

Kirk, F. G. *Total System Development for Information Systems.* New York: Wiley, 1973.

Maher, R. G. "A Common Organization Diagnostic Model and Process: Reality or Myth?" *Journal of the National Society for Performance and Instruction*, 1979, *18* (5), 17-19.

Moore, B. G., and Kondrasuk, J. "How Large Retail Chain Cut Training Costs through Centralization." *Training*, 1976, *13* (10), 48-49.

Rummler, G. A. "Human Performance Problems and Their Solutions." *Human Resources Management*, 1972, *11* (4), 2-10.

Shoemaker, H. A. "The Evolution of Management Systems for Producing Cost-Effective Training: A Bell System Experience." *Journal of the National Society for Performance and Instruction*, 1979, *18* (8), 3-7.

Smith, M. E. "Exchanging Ideas on Evaluation: 15. New England Telephone's Training Management Operational Review Plan." *Journal of the National Society for Performance and Instruction*, 1979, *18* (6), 44-47.

Smith, M. E. "Evaluating Training Operations and Programs." *Training and Development Journal*, 1980, *34* (10), 70-78.

Martin E. Smith is a training manager for the New England Telephone Company. He supervises evaluation, forecasting, and course development activities and has coauthored the most widely used training-evaluation manual in the Bell System.

Obtaining institutional support from multiple hospitals requires new approaches to identifying needs, developing educational activities, and designing political strategies for implementation.

Regionalized Continuing Medical Education: Building Multi-Institutional Support

Joseph S. Green

At the conclusion of a two-week trek to ten rural hospitals, a health professional decided that he had failed in his responsibility to educate his colleagues. He had put on almost twenty workshops over the past several months, all had been well attended, and many participants had complimented him on the programs. However, something was drastically wrong. When he visited his clients to see what was needed for future continuing education topics, he found that very few of those who had attended his lectures had been able to use the ideas. Additionally, many of the hospital directors were lukewarm about the value of the newly founded regional education center. "Why should we give up a portion of our educational monies to finance your centers, if what you do has no impact on the quality of health care at our hospital?" Obviously, a new approach was called for.

In 1972 Congress passed Public Law 92-541 which established Regional Medical Education Centers to provide continuing education for all health professionals within the Veterans Administration (VA) health care system. Each center would work with the VA hospitals and outpatient clinics within its geographic jurisdiction. The centers were staffed with fifteen-twenty health and education specialists, administrators, and support professionals.

Regional Medical Education Centers can only provide relevant, effective, and efficient continuing education, if they receive the cooperation of hospitals which employ the health professionals seeking instruction. This chapter will focus on the efforts of InterWest Regional Medical Education Center (IRMEC) in Salt Lake City, Utah, to obtain institutional support from multiple hospitals as part of the program to improve VA health care professionals' proficiency, performance, and patient care services. This was done in three steps: (1) identification of needs; (2) development of educational activities; and (3) design of political strategies for implementation.

Identification of Needs

The sources of continuing education activities ideally include needs, problems, or concerns of both health care professionals and the hospitals in which they practice (Moore and others, 1979). Without some way to identify these professional and hospital-based needs, a regional educational center would fail to gain support from the hospitals it served. The identification of needs, which represents the origin of most continuing education activities, had to accomplish two objectives: to obtain involvement in that process by key hospital staff and potential participants and to identify causes for the concerns or problems that could be addressed through educational interventions. Ideally, "the professionals involved— or some group of them—establish the standards of optimal proficiency and performance in the local setting. This same group also sets the minimal standards that can be accepted" (Houle, 1980, p. 231). Hospital management and potential participants then identify discrepancies between current and desirable practice and, as a result, have a vested interest in redressing gaps. In addition, when needs are identified in actual practice, a sound basis for evaluation of impact of the resultant continuing education has been established. Because it was initiated by those responsible for the necessary changes, the educational activity would receive strong commitment and the chances for long-term impact would be improved (Havelock and Havelock, 1973).

The InterWest RMEC decided that in order to obtain meaningful hospital support it would have to shift from passive provider of educational programs to proactive problem solver. A procedure was established to encourage each service in all thirty-three regional hospitals to identify problems and to suggest priorities for IRMEC assistance. Existing data sources within the hospital (Green and Walsh, 1979) were obtained by the IRMEC and hospital staff for use in this endeavor. All this information was funneled through the hospital's associate chief-of-staff for education and hospital leadership. Departments' suggestions were translated into hospital-wide priorities and finally, by the IRMEC staff, into regional activities for the year.

After obtaining institutional involvement, IRMEC initiated educational programs designed to assist hospital staff in the process of identifying needs and, when requested, follow-up consultant help. Finally, it was decided that when systemic deficiencies were uncovered, information would be passed on to the concerned hospitals and to their appropriate administrators. The results of all needs-identification activities and accompanying priorities were shared throughout the region. These attempts were all aimed at increasing the chances that the educational activities that would be designed would be responsive to educational needs of the organizations or their individual professionals. Institutional support from regional hospitals would only exist if it was seen that the educational activities of the center were aimed at assisting them to improve the proficiency and performance of their health professionals and the services provided to veteran-patients.

Development of Educational Activities

Once needs were identified and validated, and priorities for action set, the next tasks were to design the learning activities, select learners, and evaluate impact. In each of these areas, attempts were made to further involve professionals within member institutions.

The first decision made after the identification of needs was to select appropriate planning committees. For a given area of need, problem, or concern, only a few hospitals were involved. Planning committees were established with the following perspectives represented: potential participants, subject matter experts, and IRMEC educational process specialists. Each of the hospitals involved usually had someone representing its views on the committee. The next decision concerned the appropriate format of the educational activity. Two formats were most helpful in gaining additional support. The Traveling Health Care Consultant program was designed to bring the knowledge resources found in large hospitals affiliated with medical schools to the real-world health care problems of the isolated rural facilities (Knox, 1978). As Havelock and Havelock (1973) point out, "Of particular importance is providing training in how to continue self-training." The Train the Trainers program was aimed at extending the educational activity into actual health care practice. This program usually involved improving the proficiencies of health care professionals as supervisors, managers, or educators. Professionals would attend a regional workshop, then return to their institutions and provide similar programs for their staff.

The traditional two- or three-day workshop was still the mainstay to meet identified needs. When actual learners were selected, however, more preworkshop information was requested by the IRMEC. The aim was to obtain information from all potential participants in order to make the best match with the stated objectives. Once learners were at the workshops, additional preassessment occurred. This additional preworkshop clientele analysis was for the purposes of establishing more relevant small groups, obtaining specific real-world problems, or providing the faculty with a better understanding of their learners. Also, agenda building at the outset of conferences established priorities for upcoming educational activities and served to clarify and reinforce the objectives and identified causes of the educational needs. It was decided that inviting more than one professional from each institution gave the participants reinforcement once they were back in the hospital setting (Havelock and Havelock, 1973). For this reason, attempts were made to include more professionals from fewer hospitals, instead of one from numerous hospitals. In several workshops a variety of learning resources were made available to the learners, along with materials to take back to the practice setting. Another idea was to plan additional follow-up programs at future dates for the same learners. This allowed for attempts to apply what was learned to practice and to obtain reinforcement or to uncover additional needs.

Evaluating impact provided another opportunity for the IRMEC staff to work as facilitators of change. Many methods, such as questionnaires, telephone surveys, and on-site interviews, were used to ascertain the applicability of past educational activities. On several occasions, graduate-level studies (Richardson, Green, and Shew, 1976) were supported by the IRMEC staff as a way to better understand the nature of this impact on the health care setting. Also, the staff made personal visits to talk with past participants to find out what had and had not worked and what was needed next. In each case, where a visit was made for the purpose of evaluation, discussions were initiated with hospital leadership to better understand the health care realities and to share findings. Evaluation reports were distributed to learners and hospital leadership.

Strategies for Implementation

In order to obtain, maintain, or nurture support for the role of IRMEC within the region, two thrusts were added—one aimed at hospital directors and one targeted to provide better support for the primary vehicle for most knowledge transfer-workshops.

"There is a direct correlation between the strength of a program (as measured by size, vitality, quality of output, and support from the system) and its status in the policy-making structure" (Knowles, 1970, p. 64). In the VA health care system, power lies with individual hospital directors.

Rather than meeting socially with these individuals once a year, it was felt that they needed to be far more involved in defining the IRMEC role. To facilitate impact, the directors were invited to set priorities for yearly IRMEC activities and to attend a planning conference, held to finalize yearly plans. At these meetings, IRMEC direction, focus, and areas of emphasis were all discussed. At the conclusion, leadership of the hospitals had greater ownership of IRMEC's plan.

Another activity at this conference was to introduce directors to outstanding management and organizational development faculty and resources. Assisting those hospitals who expressed an interest in organizational development became one of the programming areas for that year. Both IRMEC staff time and resource money was made available to the hospitals. In this way the center was linking the hospitals to knowledge resource systems and providing a service that was seen by hospital management as directly beneficial.

Additionally, some hospitals expressed an interest in having the IRMEC staff visit their institutions and make suggestions about improving the relevance, effectiveness, or efficiency of their hospital-based education. These consultant activities were also seen as directly valuable to the hospitals. In the process, some indirect executive development occurred by discussing how to better organize the hospital for cost-effective continuing education. The experience of the IRMEC staff confirmed a 1978 conference on hospital-based education finding that "hospital administrators had a limited notion of the amount of education currently being conducted at the hospital and of the possibilities for improving this education" (Dunkel, 1978, p. 8). Also confirmed was the finding by Stearns and others (1974) that limited inputs by educational consultants and minimal training of hospital education staff could improve hospital-based programs.

The VA hospitals are decentralized into districts and regions. The IRMEC leadership began to meet with the hospitals' leadership on a regular basis as the latter group discussed issues and problems of common concern. The plan was to work with the directors to better integrate education as one of the problem-solving tools for management use in meeting goals to improve health care. Another suggestion under consideration was to establish an advisory committee of directors for periodic input, and to use this group to develop ways of increasing support.

To improve the chances that the typical workshop would have impact in the direction desired by the concerned hospitals, additional support was requested by IRMEC. Once workshop participants were selected, the hospital director was asked to sign the letter indicating names of the individuals he was sending and giving a promise that they would be supported when they returned and attempted to apply what they had learned. Each participant received a copy of this letter. Although this type of contract "never can guarantee success of the new role, it can help provide fundamental security and legitimacy to the role holder" (Havelock and Havelock, 1973, p. 76). For workshops that required hospital-based teams to attend and set up new programs, one of the sessions included the politics of implementation. In order for each team to develop a strategy consistent with the realities of their institutions, small group sessions were developed to discuss how to obtain hospital support for change. Finally, workshops were held at more locations outside of Salt Lake City. Sessions were planned for other major cities within the region in order to serve more individuals from the several local VA hospitals. Very little travel money was expended, and more visibility for the local hospital was obtained. Conferences were also held at many of the hospitals to increase the number of health care professionals attending from that hospital and to further bring the hospital director into IRMEC planning efforts. During many of these hospital-based programs, local educators would work with the IRMEC staff to plan, implement, and evaluate the activities. Over time, involvement of the center's staff decreased and only financial assistance was needed. When the local hospital began to share in the expenses and was intimately involved in the planning, there was a much higher probability that the resultant activity was both relevant and cost effective.

A five-year study entitled the "Hospitalwide Education and Training Project" concluded that under conditions of regionwide educational consortia, the "costs for training for the member institutions inevitably increase. Unfortunately, under these circumstances it is difficult to determine whether or not these services are less costly than if they were provided by each hospital" (Munk and Lovett, 1977, p. 58). This was the reality faced by IRMEC as it attempted to improve the nature and extent of involvement by its member hospitals to facilitate impact and obtain multi-institutional support.

A final word of caution: over the period of two years that IRMEC was attempting to change direction, it did become much more involved with efforts of the local institutions. With this increased visibility, however, came the question of unfulfilled expectations. A regional educational center must rely on the hospitals it serves for support and legitimacy. This chapter has described the strategy for developing this support.

References

Dunkel, P. *Curriculum for Educators in Health Care Institutions—Proceedings and Recommendations of an Invitational Conference.* Chicago: Hospital Research and Educational Trust, 1978.

Green, J., and Walsh, P. "Impact Evaluation in Continuing Medical Education—The Missing Link." In A. B. Knox (Ed.), *New Directions for Continuing Education: Assessing the Impact of Continuing Education,* no. 3. San Francisco: Jossey-Bass, 1979.

Havelock, R., and Havelock, M. *Training For Change Agents—A Guide to the Design of Training Programs in Education and Other Fields.* Ann Arbor: Center for Research on Utilization of Scientific Knowledge, Institute for Social Research, University of Michigan, 1973.

Houle, C. *Continuing Learning in the Professions.* San Francisco: Jossey-Bass, 1980.

Knowles, M. *The Modern Practice of Adult Education—Andragogy Versus Pedagogy.* New York: Association Press, 1970.

Knox, A. "Helping Adults to Learn." Washington, D.C.: Continuing Library Education Network and Exchange, 1978.

Moore, D., and others. "Needs Assessment for Hospital-Based Continuing Education." Paper presented at annual Associate Chief-of-Staff for Education Conference, Washington, D.C., 1979.

Munk, R., and Lovett, M. *Hospitalwide Education and Training.* Chicago: Hospital Research and Educational Trust, 1977.

Richardson, G., Green, J., and Shew, R. *Sexual Health and the Health Care Professional—An Evaluation of Impact.* Salt Lake City: InterWest Regional Medical Education Center, VA Medical Center, 1976.

Stearns, N., and others. "Impact of Program Development Consultation on Continuing Medical Education in Hospitals." *Journal of Medical Education,* 1974, *49,* 1158-1165.

Joseph S. Green was associated with the InterWest Regional Medical Education Center at the Salt Lake City Veterans Administration Medical Center between 1975 and 1979, initially as the coordinator, Instructional Design and Evaluation, and subsequently as codirector. He now is a senior staff associate at the Association of American Medical Colleges for a project to design a quality assurance program of continuing education for health professionals.

If organizational support for continuing education is to grow, someone must take the responsibility for making it happen.

A Final Note to Continuing Educators Working as Change Agents

James C. Votruba

This sourcebook has focused upon the role of the continuing educator as a change agent in strengthening support for continuing education within the larger parent organization. As such, we have examined the *process* of strengthening support in a variety of organizational settings including universities, community colleges, public schools, libraries, businesses, and complex multi-institutional systems.

Throughout our discussion, it has been clear that, if organizational support for continuing education is to be strengthened, someone must take the responsibility for making it happen. This change agent role most often falls squarely on the shoulders of the organization's continuing education administrator. While others in the organization may be willing to assist in such an effort, it is generally the continuing education administrator who must develop and articulate the vision of what needs to be accomplished and then design and manage the strategy for accomplishing it. For many continuing educators, a circumstance which makes this change agent role more difficult is that they are not in positions of central power and authority in the parent organization that they hope to change. It is therefore appropriate to close this discussion of increasing organizational support for continuing education with some suggestions to those continuing educators who are working as change agents from within.

First, *know your parent organization*. What are its norms, goals, priorities, key subsystems and key people? How does your organization function as a system? In this regard, it is vitally important to understand the organization the way it is, not the way that you wish it was or the way that you hope it someday may be.

Second, *know the external environment*. Planned change is often influenced by forces outside the organization. For example, demographic shifts, public policy trends, economic projections, market competition, and public opinion may have a dramatic impact upon the organization's view of its continuing education mission. Identify those environmental forces most likely to affect your particular change efforts and monitor them as part of your change strategy.

Third, *know your intended change inside and out*. Who and what will it affect and how? Who stands to lose and who stands to gain? What objections are liable to be raised, and what are the best responses?

Fourth, *look for allies and potential allies*. Some of them may be inside the organization, while others may be in the external community. Assess what strengths these allies bring to the change process. How might they be united to form a change team?

Fifth, *be persistent in your efforts*. Many studies suggest that successful change agents try harder and keep on trying (Havelock, 1973). However, be cautious not to let your advocacy of an idea thrust you into an adversarial relationship with the parent organization that you hope to change. Once perceived as an adversary, your influence as a change agent will diminish. You need to continually demonstrate your strong commitment to the organization while you work to adapt and change it.

Sixth, *if you have adversaries, analyze the situation from their point of view*. They may be raising some questions that you have not considered. Maybe your idea needs to be adapted to accommodate these concerns. In any event, this analysis should give you some clues regarding the nature and intensity of your opponent's concerns and whether they can be bypassed or overcome.

Seventh, *avoid impulsiveness*. Develop a strategy for accomplishing your goal and exercise a sense of timing concerning when, where, and how issues are raised. It is easy to allow your enthusiasm for the idea to cloud your sense of strategy and timing.

Eighth, *stay flexible*. It is important to have a planned change strategy but it is also important to keep in mind that it represents only a means to an end. Be sure to continually evaluate your progress in light of new information and developments. If the strategy needs changing, change it. Your change team will be valuable in assisting in this evaluation effort.

Ninth, *get help*. Strengthening organizational support for continuing education can be a difficult and complex process. If you need help, there are many places to get it. This sourcebook has identified much of the most recent literature on organizational change, and more is being written every day. In addition, there are others in similar organizations who share your commitment to continuing education. Identify these people and make plans to periodically share plans and progress. Arrange to meet at regional or national conferences, utilize conference calls, and visit each other's organizations. This "networking" with others who face similar situations can be an invaluable resource in the planned change process. In some situations you may even want to use an external consultant to help you assess the organizational environment and design a planned change strategy. Plenty of assistance is available, and it should be drawn upon when needed.

Finally, *be optimistic.* This sourcebook has demonstrated how continuing educators with vision and purpose have strengthened support for continuing education within their parent organizations. It is not always easy and it requires proficiency, but it can be done and there are lots of potential adult participants who are counting on you to succeed. Indeed, if we are to become a truly lifelong learning society, you *must* succeed. Good luck!

Reference

Havelock, R. G. *The Change Agent's Guide to Innovation in Education.* Englewood Cliffs, N.J.: Educational Technology Publications, 1973.

James C. Votruba is associate director of the Office of Continuing Education and Public Service and assistant professor of both continuing education and higher education, University of Illinois at Urbana-Champaign.

Index

A

Administrators: as change agents, 105-107; coordination by, 8-9; as interpreters, 33-34; leadership by, 2, 9-10; split appointment of, 5; in university, importance of, 32
Admissions, and agency-organization relationships, 3-4
Adult Independent Learning Project, 84, 85, 86, 87
Agarivala-Rogers, R., 15, 28
Agencies: characteristics of, 2-3; facilities, equipment, and supplies for, 6; financing, 5-6, 8; inputs to, 3-6; in noneducational organizations, 2, 6, 7; and outcomes, 9; policies and procedures of, 5; and process, 6-9; and program development, 7-8; relationships of, with parent organizations, 1-11; staff for, 4-5
American Association of Community and Junior Colleges, Center for Community Education at, 62
American Library Association, 83
Argyris, C., 15, 27
Averill, D., 52, 56

B

Baille, D., 52, 26
Baldridge, J. V., 17, 28, 30, 35
Beder, H. W., 65-71
Bell, C., 25, 28
Benefits: of faculty rewards system, 47-48, to public schools, 66-69; publishing, 69; of student services, 55
Berridge, R. I., 75-76, 78
Bowser, R. D., 93, 95
Brawer, F. B., 58, 63
Brown, M. A., 4, 10

C

California, programs for older adults in, 76, 77
Catalyst, as leader, 26, 53
Centra, J. A., 43, 50

Change: approaches to, 13-18; capacity for, 22; combined approach to. 17-20; and compatibility, 22-23; design for, 18, 20-24; goals of, 20; guidelines for, 106-107; human problem solving approach to, 15-16; implementing, 54-56; and leadership, 21, 26-27; and linkage, 17-19, 21; managing, 24-27; and openness, 21-22; organization of, 21; ownership of, 24; political approach to, 16-17; psychological dimension of, 15-16; rational planning approach to, 14-15; and rewards, 23; social interaction approach to, 15; strategies for, 13-28, 51-53, 83-84, 85-86, 93-94; and synergy, 23-24; team for, 25-26
Chellino, S. N., 90, 95
Chicago, University of, 31
Clark, D., 14, 28
College Entrance Examination Board, Office of Library Independent Study and Guidance Projects of, 84
Colleges. *See* Community colleges; Universities
Committee on Institutional Cooperation, 48
Community based, concept of, 59
Community colleges: characteristics of, 57-58, as community based, 58-63; continuing education in, 57-63; evaluation in, 61-62, and needs assessment, 61; parent organization relationships of, 3, 6; planning in, 59-60; programs in, 60-61; resources for, 62-63
Compatibility: and change, 22-23; of faculty rewards, 46; and financial support, 40
Conroy, B., 81-88
Consortium for Public Library Innovation, 84-85, 87
Continuing education: admission to, 3-4; agency for, in relationship with

109

Continuing education: (continued) parent organization, 1-11; benefits of, 66-69; change in, 13-28, 105-107; and colleagueship within university, 34; in community colleges, 57-63; coordination of, 76-77; by corporations, 89-95; external support for, 32-33, 67, 70-71; faculty rewards for, 43-50; financing, 37-42; gaining support for, 77-78; initiation of, 75-76; in libraries, 81-88; medical, 97-103; network for, 5, 48, 107; for older adults, 73-79; organizational style of, 30-31; principles for, 34-35; in public schools, 65-71; resistance to, 29-30; and students services, 51-56; in universities, 29-35

Cooperative Extension Service, parent organization relationships of, 2, 3

Copeland, H., 4, 10

Corporations: agency relationships of, 2, 3-4, 5-6; continuing education in, 89-95; decentralization in, 89-90; reorganization of, 90-93

Council on Library Resources, 84

Credibility: in corporate continuing education, 94; of planned change team, 25; and student services, 53

Curtis, D. V., 35

D

Dahl, D. A., 37-42
Darkenwald, G., 10, 66, 69, 71
Decision makers, preferences and styles of, 55
DeProspo, E. R., 84, 85, 87-88
Dinneen, M., 90, 95
DiSilvestro, F., 53, 56
Duncan, R., 16, 28
Dunkel, P., 101, 102

E

Easton, D., 16, 28
Ecker, G., 35
Education Act, Title V of, 78
Eignor, D., 52, 56

F

Faculty: outcomes of reward project for, 48-49; project on rewards for, 45-58; rewards to, for continuing education, 43-50

Farmer, J. A., Jr., 30, 35
Farmer, M., 52, 56
Financial support: of agencies, 5-6, 8; and compatibility, 40; of continuing education, 37-42; and opinion leaders, 39-40; and ownership, 40-41; in public schools, 68; social systems approach to, 38-41; for student services, 55; traditional approach to, 37-38

Florida, Community Instructional Service in, 61
French, W., 25, 28
Fricke, N. W., 73, 78
Fund for Adult Education, 83, 85, 86, 87

G

Gleazer, E. J., Jr., 58, 63
Gollattscheck, J. F., 57-63
Gordon, M., 44, 50
Green, J. S., 97-103
Guba, E., 14, 28

H

Hanna, D. E., 43-50
Harlacher, E. L., 63
Harper, W. R., 31
Havelock, M., 98, 99, 100, 102-103
Havelock, R. G., 13, 17-19, 26, 28, 46, 50, 53, 54, 56, 98, 99, 100, 102-103, 106, 107
Havighurst, R., 52, 56
Hewitt, C. H., 83, 87
Hohenstein, W. V., 43, 50
Hospitals, continuing education in, 97-103
Houle, C. O., 4, 10, 98, 103

I

Illinois, University of, at Urbana-Champaign, Faculty Reward Project at, 44-49
InterWest Regional Medical Education Center (IRMEC), 98-102

J

Jones, J., 25, 28

K

Kahn, R. L., 3, 10
Katz, D., 3, 10
Kirk, F. G., 94, 95
Knapp, S. E., 30
Knight, D. M., 81, 87
Knowles, M., 100, 103
Knox, A. B., 1-11, 30, 35, 43, 44, 50, 52, 56, 66, 69, 71, 99, 103
Kondrasuk, J., 93, 95
Kotter, J., 21, 28

L

Lake, D. B., 62, 63
Lawrence, P., 21, 28
Leadership: by agency administrators, 2, 9-10; and change, 21, 26-27; characteristics of, 26; roles in, 26-27, 53-54
Lee, C. C., 15, 28
Leigh, D., 81, 87
Libraries: agency relationships of, 2, 6; change projects in, 82-86; continuing education in, 81-88; issues for, 86-87; roles of, 81-82; and self-directed learners, 84-85
Library Services and Construction Act, 87
Lindquist, J., 13, 14, 15, 17, 18, 20n, 21, 25, 28, 46, 50, 54, 56, 60
Linkages: and change, 17-19, 21; for faculty rewards, 48
Litwak, E., 67, 71
Lorsch, J., 21, 28
Los Angeles, program for older adults in, 74, 77
Lovett, M., 102, 103

M

McCarthy, M. B., 43, 44, 50
McClenney, B., 62, 63
Maher, R. G., 94, 95
Marshall, M. G., 73-79
Martin, A. B., 81, 87
Mavor, A. S., 84, 85, 87-88
Mayer, H., 67, 71
Medical education: continuing, 97-103; development of activities for, 99-100; implementation strategies in, 100-102; needs identification in, 98-99

Mezirow, J., 10, 66, 69, 71
Michael, D. N., 35
Michigan, University of, Center for Research on the Utilization of Scientific Knowledge at, 13
Miles, M., 25, 28
Military services, agency relationships of, 4
Miller, P. A., 29-35
Moore, B. G., 93, 95
Moore, D., 98, 103
Munk, R., 102, 103

N

National Advisory Council on Adult Education, 76-77, 78
National Center for Higher Education Management Systems, 62
National Commission on Libraries and Information Science, 82, 88
National Council on Aging, 78
National Council on Community Services and Continuing Education, 63
National Endowment for the Humanities, 82, 84
Needs assessment: for community colleges, 61; for medical education, 98-99; for older adults, 74-75
Networks: for change agents, 5, 107; for faculty rewards project, 48
New Jersey, public school support for continuing education in, 66
New York, public school support for continuing education in, 67
Nourse, E. S., 81, 87

O

Older adults: establishing programs for, 73-79; needs of, 74-75; number of, 73, 74
Opinion leaders: for faculty rewards, 46-47; and medical education, 98, 100-101
Orr, B., 52, 56
Outreach, defined, 76-77
Ownership: and change, 24; in corporate continuing education, 92, 94; of faculty rewards, 46-47; and financial support, 40-41

P

Parent organization: agency relationship with, 1-11; community colleges as, 57-63; corporations as, 89-95; demands and constraints of, 6; dynamics of, 1-3; hospitals as, 97-103; library as, 81-88; principles of, 66; public school as, 65-79; university as, 29-56
Parsons, T., 15, 28
Patton, C. V., 43, 44, 50
Porter, L., 52, 56
President, of university, importance of, to continuing education, 31-32
Prisons, agency relationships of, 4
Process helper, as leader, 27, 53-54
Professional association, agency relationships of, 4, 6
Public Law 92-541, 97
Public school: agency relationships of, 3, 4, 5; benefits to, 66-69; continuing education disruption to, 68-69; establishing programs in, 73-79; and fallback strategy, 70-71; support from, 65-71

R

Reeves, M., 30, 35
Regional Medical Education Centers, 97-102
Reilly, A., 25, 28
Religious institutions, agency relationships of, 2, 6, 7
Resource linker, as leader, 27, 54
Rewards: and change, 23; to faculty, for continuing education, 43-50
Rice, R. L., 90, 95
Richardson, G., 100, 103
Riggs, J. A., 51-56
Riley, G. L., 35
Roberts, E., 63
Robinson, E., 15, 28
Rogers, M. E., 15, 18
Rosnow, R., 15, 28
Rummler, G. A., 93, 95

S

Schlesinger, L., 21, 28
Schon, D. A., 15, 27
Seldin, P., 43, 50
Sheehy, G., 56
Shew, R., 100, 103
Shoemaker, F. F., 15, 28
Shoemaker, H. A., 91, 95
Simerly, R. G., 37-42
Smith, F., 66, 67, 71
Smith, M. E., 89-95
Solution giver, as leader, 26-27, 53
Southern California, University of, student services at, 52
Staff, and agency-organization relationship, 4-5
Stearns, N., 101, 103
Student services: change strategy for, 51-53; for continuing education, 51-56; implementing changes in, 54-56

T

Tadlock, M., 59-60, 63
Team: factors in forming, 25-26; for faculty rewards, 46; for planned change, 25-26; for student services, 52-53
Title I, and programs for older adults, 74
Toro, J. O., 84, 85, 87-88

U

U.S. Office of Education, 73, 82, 84
U.S. Senate Special Committee on Aging, 73, 78
Universities: agency relationships of, 3-4, 5; continuing education in, 29-35; faculty rewards in, 43-50; financial support from, 37-42; history of, 30; principles in, 34-35; strengthening support from, 31-5; student services in, 51-56

V

Van Hise, C., 31
Veterans Administration, 97-102
Votruba, J. C., vii-viii, 13-28, 43, 44, 46, 50, 105-107

W

Walsh, P., 98, 102
Watson, G., 15, 28
White House Conference on Aging, 73, 76
Wisconsin, University of, 31
Wygal, B. R., 63

Z

Zaltman, G., 16, 28